Asilomar Retreat Center,
Monterey California 1986

HOW TO GAIN
NOTHING
FROM
BUDDHIST
PRACTICE

DARREN LITTLEJOHN
BESTSELLING AUTHOR OF THE 12-STEP BUDDHIST

How to Gain Nothing from Buddhist Practice:

A practitioner's guide to end suffering.

by Darren Littlejohn

For permissions contact: darrenblittlejohn@gmail.com

Cover by Kostis Pavlou.

Ebook ISBN: 978-0-9895260-2-9

Print ISBN: 978-0-9895260-3-6

Library of Congress Control Number: 2016954065

For Zippy and Mackie.
May we always find each other.

The Buddha was asked skeptically,

"What have you gained through meditation?"

The Buddha replied, "Nothing at all."

"Then, Blessed One, what good is it?"

"Let me tell you what I lost through meditation: sickness, anger, depression, insecurity, the burden of old age, the fear of death.

That is the good of meditation, which leads to nirvana."

TABLE OF CONTENTS

FOREWORD

There are many dharma doors and they were not all taught a long time ago. New dharma doors open every day and when we learn to look we find them everywhere. A dharma door is a way of looking out that lets you look in and lets you see that outside and inside are not so different.

Since we were born we have each had many different experiences: some we think of as happy and some we think of as sad. Whatever their flavour, the key thing is that something was happening and in particular, something was happening for me. I was there and now I am here. Events, both objective and subjective, pass yet somehow we are always here. We are not apart from our life, not a neutral observer. Our life is not something that is happening to us, but rather who we take ourselves to be is an inseparable part of the unfolding of existence.

The noise of the neighbors in their back garden, the feeling of anxiety when you realise you are late for work, all such events are also reminders that we are here, alive! The event and my response to it arise together, not as two linked things but as a wave in the co-emergent field.

Of course the more obsessional we are the more the content of the experience seems important. "Do I have enough cigarettes to get me through the night?" Our need for objects to reassure us is a sign that we are a bit out of balance.

If we are too tilted towards towards the object then we get lost in stuff and consumerist capitalism ensures there is always more stuff to get. If we are too tilted towards the subject we get engrossed in our private flow of hopes and fears, memories and plans. Buddhism offers many ways of finding the middle way that negotiates all extremes and polarities.

This book sets out key Buddhist principles and practices in a way that demonstrates their practical relevance in our everyday life. We all need help because basically we are not isolated individuals but part of the world. Giving and receiving help is a pulsation as simple as breathing in and out. The question is, "What is it truly safe to rely on?" Buddhist practice begins with refuge. By relying on the Buddha we find ourselves and when we find ourselves we get a new sense of what we might need from the world. The ego's desperation and capacity to cling on to anything easily has us pursuing objects and goals that will lead us astray, away from the chance to find ourselves. This book offers a deep dharma door that opens onto the home that we have never left. -James Low, author of *Simply Being: Texts in the Dzogchen Tradition*

Praise for How to Gain Nothing from Buddhist Practice

Simple steps to combine breath-work & compassion to alleviate our experience of pain in life.

-Erik Pema Kunsang, Dzogchen Deity Practice: Meeting Your True Nature, Translator for Tulku Urgyen Rinpoche

In this eminently readable and practical overview of the Buddhist path, Darren Littlejohn presents the core teachings in a way that reverberates with our present situation. As Littlejohn makes clear, Buddhism does not offer us anything we don't already possess. We have nothing to gain and everything to lose – most importantly, our suffering and its causes – by following this experiential roadmap to the freedom of groundlessness and non-attachment.

-Lama Marut, author of A Spiritual Renegade's Guide to the Good Life and Be Nobody

After reading How to Gain Nothing, you may ask yourself what did I just read? And then either laugh or cry. Because Darren LittleJohn with great wit, humour,

4

and dharma knowledge will empty your mind. This excellent book will tell you all you need to know about the Dharma, and then the rest is up to you.

-Valerie Mason-John, author of Eight Step Recovery
Using the Buddha's teachings to overcome addiction

Darren's writing and teaching is integrative in a way that is sorely needed by a culture struggling to make sense of the universality of suffering. When the solutions presented for people in recovery are presented as solutions for all beings, we transcend the stigma and limited effectiveness associated with traditional approaches to addiction. Darren's work does just that, in an accessible and engaging way.

-Buster Ross, MA, CADC II, LPC, CSC and
Adjunct and Course Developer at Hazelden Betty
Ford Graduate School of Addiction Studies.

"I've long admired Darren Littlejohn's candidness as a human being and as a writer. In "How to Gain Nothing from Buddhist Practice" Littlejohn gives you some of his most candid reflections to date about the nature of suffering and the path to overcome it. Written with an accessibility and humanity that even the non-Buddhists

among us can appreciate and value, this is Littlejohn's best book to date!"

-Jamie Marich, Ph.D., author of Dancing Mindfulness: A Creative Path for Healing and Transformation, and Trauma and the Twelve Steps: A Complete Guide to Recovery Enhancement

We live in a world where getting something—money, power, prestige— is the very definition of success. Yet in that worldly success, few have found lasting peace and happiness. In his latest book, How to Gain Nothing from Buddhist Practice Darren Littlejohn uses ancient teachings in a fresh and modern way that is sure to inspire. A must read for Buddhists and non Buddhists alike!

-Darren Main, Author of Yoga and the Path of the Urban Mystic and The River of Wisdom: Reflections on Yoga, Meditation, and Mindful Living

PREFACE

"It is impossible to attain the twofold purity of Buddhahood or to realize fully the truth of emptiness without completing the two accumulations of merit and wisdom. As it says in the sutras, 'Until one has completed the two sacred accumulations, One will never realize sacred emptiness.'" -Patrul Rinpoche, *Words of My Perfect Teacher*

We all start with the desire to get something from our practice. It's true, this book is about the how and why of practicing as a Buddhist. The teaching of The Two Accumulations instructs us in how to "gain" merit and wisdom. But the Dharma (teaching) is never what we think it is. There are so many words spoken, innumerable explanations, positions and arguments among practitioners. But what is the real meaning and how do we begin to understand it in a way that makes our lives better, right now? These are the topics considered here.

Before I go on, thanks for buying this book. My name is Darren Littlejohn; I'm a recovering drug addict with over 18 years sober, a fledgling Buddhist practitioner for 30+ years, and introductory yoga teacher for almost 6 years. First of all, you're not going to get what you expect from me. I just want to let you know that.

You're going to get something different. Before we go into how to do different meditation sessions, I'll ask you to consider some readings and some questions.

This book is based on a talk that I gave online for Worldwide Insight for people in recovery from addictions who also have an interest in Buddhism. My talks are almost always spontaneous meditations. The freedom of speech in that medium doesn't convert perfectly to the written word. As I listened and read the transcript, this work—like everything that we allow to be created in the natural way that it wants—needed to unfold. It asked to be shaped and refined. Some ideas had to be dropped, others expanded.

You'll find here variations on meditations that I teach frequently in my yoga classes. You can find recordings of these on the-12stepbuddhist.com and on The 12-Step Buddhist podcast as well as gainnothing.com. This book is not specifically geared towards people in recovery. But I'm in recovery and have written extensively about it, so people in recovery or who might be thinking about recovery will relate. The meditations that I teach to my yoga students are the ones that I've generally been focusing on. These are all based in Buddhist meditation techniques, integrated with yoga methods.

Who Wants to Read About Nothing?

If you suffer, this book is for you. You don't have to be Buddhist, but if you are you'll still learn something here. This is an unconventional book.

When writers write and marketers create products and brands, they do something called an Empathy Map. That's where you get inside the head of the intended audience to understand their challenges so that you can offer solutions that help them. This builds value in the books, products, services.

One of the main things that you're supposed to understand in the empathy map is the *pain point*. Where does it hurt? How is your customer, reader or client suffering?

From a Buddhist view, we learn to touch our own suffering so that we can create empathy and compassion for others. I have touched my own suffering. I'll tell you some stories in this book that will make that clear. The point is that I understand the suffering of being human. I work very hard to stay afloat and do the right thing so that I can ultimately provide value to you, my reader.

The Buddha taught the First Noble Truth: Life is suffering.

Your pain point is my pain point.

My product, if you will, is my experience in applying teachings to my own suffering and that of those around me. In 12-Step communities we say that, "No matter how far down the scale we have gone, we will see how our experience can benefit others." I'll teach you my understanding of what the Buddha taught to liberate ourselves from suffering. I share through my own experience. I hope it helps you.

Remember, you're the hero of this journey. All I am is a voice in your head as you read this. You'll have to learn to listen to your own *inner Dharma coach* as you develop your intuition in practice.

How to Gain Nothing From This Book

I'm going to teach you how to meditate from a lot of different angles. Contrary to what you may have heard, there are infinite angles from which to begin. Where appropriate, I've added some suggestions for journaling, reflection and further meditation. The reason that I ask you to pause and do some reflection is that it takes more than words to understand the teachings. I've spoken for hours on retreats and in workshops, thinking I was crystal clear the whole time and that everyone was getting it. But when I quizzed the group, I found out that students were overwhelmed with the amount of information and unfamiliar with the Dharma being presented. Over the years, I've learned to break things down into smaller chunks, and ask people to pause and reflect on them before skipping ahead.

Some sections are labeled, "Journal." These are probably best suited for you to write about. But you could just sit with the question if you prefer. Most chapters include meditation questions. These are meant to be considered as you sit in your meditation position for a designated period of time. But you could write about them instead. Or you could do both. Or you could go back and forth any way that you like. You might walk around as you reflect, or think about these things before you take a nap.

But do come back to the questions. Work on them for the rest of your life, or skip them until they wake you up in the middle of your dream.

I use terms in this book such as *meditation, yoga, Dharma, prana, pranayama* and *kundalini*. You may have some familiarity with these concepts and practices. The way I use these words is probably different than what you've heard before. Use your open mind to consider meanings. Unfreeze your thinking. I've included a glossary at the end of the book for quick reference.

The good news about there being nothing to gain is that there's also nothing to lose. That said you've got everything to gain (knowledge, wisdom) and nothing to lose (there was never anyone there in the first place) or nothing to gain (because you can't add to your real reality) and everything to lose (pain, suffering in an endless cycle) by stepping onto a path of meditation, reflection and clarification.

How to Create the Community that You Crave

One of the most common questions I get is how to find others to connect with on the path. Many people live in areas where Buddhist organizations are rare or nonexistent. If you go to the book website gainnothing.com, you can download a free guide to start your own meditation group. The last chapter gives you practices along those lines so you'll know how to follow the guide. Here are a few more suggestions for building community.

- Buy a copy of this book for a friend

- Head to your favorite online retailer for the version of the book you want to gift. On some you can click a "Give as Gift" button. You can choose to e-mail the e-book gift to the recipient with a future delivery date, or print out a voucher (which you can then place in a greeting card).

- Share your progress, questions, practices. Mention this book on your social media. Use the hastags #gainnothing #howtogainnothing

- Join our Facebook Community for support and inspiration. https://www.facebook.com/gainnothing/

- Join the *sangha* on gainnothing.com.

I hope that you find meaning in this work until the search for meaning becomes meaningless.

-d

Darren Littlejohn

San Diego, CA

April, 2016

ACKNOWLEDGEMENTS

I appreciate the work of my editor, Zach Larson, who was kind and clear. My hands are together as I bow to my Dzogchen Master Chogyal Namkhai Norbu Rinpoche, whose Sutra, Tantra and Dzogchen Transmissions dispel all confusion about Dharma. I appreciate the years of support of all of my friends on Facebook, Twitter, Instagram. I'm especially grateful to my early readers: Inna, Amber, and Rick.

CHAPTER ONE

THE THREE POISONS

"Dzogchen is said to be based on the real meaning because right from the beginning it teaches one to find oneself in one's natural condition without changing or altering it."

- Chogyal Namkhai Norbu Rinpoche,
Dzogchen: The Self-Perfected State

There is No Foundation

I'd love to start by setting up a foundation for you to understand Buddhism. But ultimately, there is no foundation. There is nothing to grasp, no place to put your feet and nothing to hold on to. Does that scare you? It scares me. We're so afraid of not existing like we think we do. The thought of nothingness can be quite terrifying. In fact, some Buddhists freak out at the idea. When my first book came out, I gave a talk at a pretty serious Tibetan Buddhist group in Sacramento. The teacher there, from a conservative Tibetan tradition, commented that he almost lost it when I started talking about emptiness. They usually take a while to introduce that topic to their students. But the experience of and immersion in the sheer, total, immeasurable expanse of nothing is, in fact, the ultimate goal of the first teachings of the Buddha.

Buddhists who follow this path don't really talk about nothingness as the destination, but that's really the ultimate conclusion of the first of the Buddha's teachings. The way to get to this non-place with no path and no one to arrive is through renunciation of worldly concerns. It's a hard path and it takes many lifetimes. Why is that?

Because our karma is very, very heavy. And because we're so afraid. We cling. We clutch. We hold on by our fingernails. We create a fictitious reality that we think can hold on to. The last thing we really want to do is let it all dissolve, like a dream that dissipates into the morning light. What we really want is to fix everything. Put ourselves on top. Make it better. Feel better. Not just better, but fantastic. And if we can't feel better, we don't want other people to remind us of how we feel. We medicate, distract, blame, project. We want life to be something other than what it is. We're convinced that it should be different. But it's not, and we hate it.

I'll give you an example. This morning I was walking my elderly dog when I was stricken with a deep sadness over the loss of our other dog. He and his friend Zippy were very close, inseparable in fact. Zippy died of heart failure about a year ago. I thought about how badly I missed Zippy and felt so bad for my Mackie because I know his little heart is broken. He misses his friend and I miss my friend and I can do nothing to stop the pain for either of us. That made me feel powerless. Furious. Yet that is how it is. Our friend died. We can't bring him back like the redheaded witch lady brought back Jon Snow on *Game of Thrones*. So what are we left with? We're left with life, just as it is, in this moment.

This is the practice. Nothing concrete or substantial *actually* exists, especially our thoughts, beliefs and feelings. The more we hold on, the more acutely we suffer. In fact, the tighter we hold on to the notion that we shouldn't suffer, the worse it gets. We suffer. That's what Buddha said. Anyone care to argue that point?

So, now that we have that fundamental idea, what do we do? Depends on who you ask and what strain of Dharma they're following. Yes, it may surprise you, but there are different views on how to deal with the main problem of suffering within each system of Buddhism and its interpretation of what Buddha said. Sound familiar? The same could be said of Catholics and Protestants and many other sects and traditions.

Buddhism, like most systems, has many variations. Within each there are some purists and fundamentalists and hard liners. There are others that live in the essence of the teachings and are more relaxed. You might have met some Buddhists who aren't much fun. I'm not one of those. I'm really fun, in case you were wondering.

That said, the ideas that you'll read about in *Gain Nothing* could upset some purists. Should we argue? My advice is this: if discussing ideas that are different or threatening or weird to the person you're trying to discuss them with, don't discuss them with that person. Perhaps find someone to discuss them with who is interested in that type of discussion. Readers of my work have a website with a member's area, a Facebook community and a format for local meditation groups that can be used to collaborate with other like-minded souls. Feel free to use those resources. But don't go out on a mission to convince anyone of anything. It's quite pointless. Alternately, you could just sit alone and not worry about connecting with others. That is totally up to you. Some practitioners have gone into lifetime solitary retreat for that very reason.

There's a lot to forget about Buddhism, but it's important to learn it first. We don't have space here to go into all of the similarities and differences of the different Dharma tribes and I don't have comprehensive knowledge of all those details. I don't think any one person does. Buddha would. But I haven't seen him around lately. I follow teachings and the teachings are about the essence. We'll get into that as we go. Maybe you're starting to feel it already. Or not. But if you do the practices that I suggest, something's bound to shift. You may touch emptiness. You might, in fact, gain nothing.

These are my views, based on teachings that I've received and a lifetime of experience. If you meditate on what I'm sharing with you here, I'm confident that you'll find it to be useful. I only share things that work for me. These tools have great value. It's up to you to learn, meditate, apply and realize. No one can do it for you. Not even The Buddha.

What are the takeaways about Buddhism then? The main thing that you need to know about Buddhism is that the Buddha taught about three things that keep us suffering: **attachment, ignorance, and aversion**. We hold on to some things, push other things away and are clueless as to what's really going on. If you really understood the nature of suffering and lived by that understanding, you'd be enlightened. I'm not enlightened, so I keep working on this stuff. I'm just a total geek about Dharma and have been into it for decades. Whether this is your first exposure to it or if you're a well seasoned old-fart practitioner, my intention is to help you understand it better for yourself. If I miss the mark for you, then of course you can read one of the hundreds of watered down books about mindfulness that come out every year.

Buddhism, in all its forms and lineages, promises a path out of suffering. But that doesn't mean we reject suffering. This is one of those spiritual paradoxes that has to be experienced. Though we use our minds to understand the tools, we know that ultimately, to make any progress and no progress, the tools are to be abandoned. Learn it, live it, let it go. Just like our lives. We all come to our final resting points in time.

Suffering is Optional?

My old AA sponsor used to say, "Suffering is optional." It's not pain, but our resistance to it that causes it to run deeper. A friend in recovery who also had a mastectomy for breast cancer told me that she'd like to know if someone had a body part removed like she did, if they'd still think suffering was optional. 12-Step indeed has the tendency to oversimplify problems and solutions. But I think what they're getting at is that we tend to amplify our suffering with our mental reactions to it. I would never tell a sick person that they're making themselves suffer. But I would try to help them find relief, perhaps by teaching them how to not add to the suffering.

We have an experience. We react with tension and thought that intensifies the experience. Samsara is a cycle. The cycle can be broken. One way that we can break the cycle is by focusing on our breath. I'll give you some practices here in a bit.

Another adage in recovery is that pain is the "touchstone of all spiritual growth." That means that in order to grow, we really need to experience some adversity. We need to suffer to make powerful shifts in our spiritual consciousness. That's not to say that we should suffer, but that suffering is a prerequisite to spiritual development. We don't just walk into the store and buy spiritual progress or click and have it delivered same-day from an online store. We must pay dues.

One day as I was explaining the complications of my suffering to my therapist, he offered an explanation as to why it always seems to happen the way it does for me. I had been saying how it's so bizarre that in some areas, my life was magical and in others, it was ridiculous in terms of the amount of struggle I had to go through. He said that we all had to pay a price to walk the earth and that this was my price. The things that I had to take care of in the course of my life are my tithing. It's sort of like the cost of living in San Diego. We have great weather, and our costs for basic things are a bit high compared to less sunny locations. We refer to it as our sunshine tax. My taxes (sufferings) are high for getting to do the things I love; live in the sun, teach yoga, have a beautiful wife, write books and be sober.

And just because we have paid our dues doesn't mean we're automatically going to grow spiritually. There are plenty of people on the street outside my building here in Downtown San Diego who have paid and are paying their dues of suffering, but don't appear to be in any sort of growth pattern. From my point of view, it looks more like a steady decline into deeper suffering, with no end in sight.

We must suffer to grow and we must find wisdom in the suffering. Otherwise it's just a disgusting waste.

A therapist friend of mine suggests that all emotions are rooted in pain or suffering. They're all connected and interrelated facets of each other.

The Buddha also taught about interdependence. That means that everything is related. Nothing and no one exists in a vacuum.

If all emotions derive from the same stem, then all feelings are petals of the same lotus. Our linear minds tend to impose logic onto emotions, but emotions are like dream states, deep beneath our conscious surface. This is one reason why meditation opens wounds and another reason why breath meditation is a way to heal emotions as they surface. Our brains try to make meaning from feelings. We feel that we must feel a certain way, not the way we're feeling. This is the viewpoint that causes suffering because we deny reality. That isn't natural and takes us out of the flow. The more we sit in opposition to what is, the harder what is is for us. Because it is what it is. It's not something else.

In Buddhamind, instead of being in opposition, we sit calmly in the center of all experience as it arises. We feel it, allow it to liberate and let it go. Everything is happening right now. Our awareness is usually tunnel visioned. We can't possibly be aware of everything or our minds would explode. But Buddhamind really is aware of everything, all at once, not just in our own psyches but in the minds of all beings who are alive, who have ever been conscious or who will ever live. That's why some teachers call it Big Mind. In order to handle it we must be in a relaxed state, opposing nothing.

We cannot comprehend infinite God with our finite selves, says AA literature. Buddhism doesn't acknowledge a "Creator God."

But Buddhamind is infinite. It is who we really are. We can bring our minds to the place where we can look in that mirror, and recognize our real nature.

Why You Suffer: Attachment

We're always grasping to some idea, person, process or object, or we're looking for something shiny and new to grasp onto. From Buddha's perspective, we're all attached. It's easy to understand. It's not easy to fix.

For example, have you ever tried to let go of something, like a long standing resentment or a childhood fear? Let's explore that together as we practice. If you can't taste attachment in the back of your throat, there's no point in going any further.

Relationships are one of the easiest ways to get attached. Sometimes we get superglued to another person. We might even be codependent. If you don't like that term, you can just think of it as a form of attachment to people.

Seven Signs That You Could Be Attached

- Are you in denial about unhealthy relationship dynamics?
- Are you a bit over-controlling?
- Tend to be a little obsessed?
- Emotionally repressed?
- Do you have low self-worth?
- Have difficulty communicating your needs?
- Do you have weak personal boundaries?

Codependency\person attachment may appear at first glance to be limited to dealing with addicts who are still active in addiction. My own experience is that the dynamics of codependency can be a subtle part of any intimate relationship. In my 19th year of recovery, I am still prone to be codependent. Typically codependency is thought of as being stuck with an addicted spouse. But it comes up and in a lot of ways and looks different than that. The dynamics can come up for any of us, and they cause pain.

Al-anon family groups say that when it comes to the other person's sickness, be it addiction, mental illness or whatever, we have to remember the Three Cs.

- We didn't cause it

- We can't control it

- We sure as hell can't cure it

Much of my time is spent in service to people who want soul-help. I really feel people's energy. It's a gift-and a curse. Sometimes I don't know that it's not mine because I feel the other person's karma so strongly. Whether it's teaching yoga or meditation, writing books and blogs or answering phones, my time is often spent trying to help people heal. My boundaries are usually pretty good. But sometimes it's easy to get caught up in what I think is in the best interest of others. When that happens, I usually joke that "I'm not 'co,' I'm just concerned." But I can get as sick as anybody else when you get right down to it. I can get fixated on the way others are acting and lose focus on who I am because I sometimes forget not to base my self-worth on the actions of others.

Sometimes my energy is low or I have an off day. That makes me vulnerable to thinking that the feelings of others are my own. Old tapes, such as self-loathing, start spinning in my head. Before I know it, I feel depressed, angry or upset. This kind of attachment can create a seemingly endless loop of suffering. It comes from our childhood mostly. Our childhood happens the way it does due to the karma that we brought into this life from the past. When people who we "love" don't do what we want, our buttons get pushed and we react. It's really hard to quiet the sound of our old tapes when those around us are playing theirs through loudspeakers. It's almost as if we're all playing our songs and no one's listening to each other. That is the noise of samsara. That's why couples counseling is all about listening skills. Meditation is about listening to our innermost selves which can then translate to listening to others. These practices will help you and your relationships, especially when combined with a multi-modal approach.

Journal Practice

Write about three experiences that you've had trouble letting go of. These could be relationship-oriented, or something else. Write about the seven signs listed above in relation to your attachment so you can get a super clear feeling of what will come up for you as you practice.

Then, consider the following for any areas of attachment:

- Who is in charge of what you hold onto?

- What does it mean to grasp mentally or emotionally?

- What would letting go feel like?

Why You Suffer: Ignorance

One of my teachers, Lama Khemsar Rinpoche, is fond of saying, "You don't know what you don't know." You know, it's really hard to tell people about a state of being beyond concepts. The Buddha tried. Many masters teach tirelessly in an effort to reveal a path out of suffering. But can we really listen if our minds are totally distracted? How can we hear the teaching if we're caught up in an endless torrents of thoughts that dominate our minds? If we can hear something useful and understand just a little how to apply it, maybe we can get somewhere, if there's anywhere to get *to*.

In a conventional sense, ignorance means we're not aware of something. Can you see where the teachings of the Buddha are the opposite of ignorance? In time and space, we're constantly bombarded with stimuli. Where could we possibly go to get a little quiet? If we did find such a sanctuary, would the noises in our mind erupt like a fighter jet blasting through our heads amidst that silence?

Let's do a little meditation to invite awareness to the infinite space within, even though there is no in and there is no out.

Meditation

Have a nice straight back and comfortable seat. Find still presence. That is the entire practice.

Just like a sheet drifting to the bed, we fall into place, allow ourselves to spread out a little bit energetically. We're really training the *global mind*. This is a vast sense of awareness. It is the opposite of ignorance. Yoga is meditation and meditation is yoga and it is an inner game. The *inner game of yoga* is that balance between our awareness and our activity. We slow the physical activity in our seated meditation position.

You'll notice as you meditate that there's energetic activity, mental movement. The idea that there's always something more to gain is one that we can loosen our grasp on. Do we have to replace it with an idea that we already have everything we need? I don't know. I probably could use another cup of coffee. I've got some things to do. But really being *in* this present moment, I allow myself to experience my life as it is. Just notice that compulsion, that fixation, the grasping. The very, very best I can do even if I'm an ultra skilled meditator would be to notice that I'm really grasping. I'm quite a grasper. Actually, I'm clutching constantly. So we just notice that.

We can invite our awareness to those places in the physical body where we might be manifesting tension. You would be hard-pressed to be in your physical body without manifesting an expression of your mental, emotional state. If we could do something like this, we would truly be practitioners of yoga. Remember, yoga is the inner practice, not just some postures. It's the joining of deep relaxation and all activity. In the inner game of meditation, we're constantly working with this balance between our awareness and our compulsion. I see myself grasping. This is an important point to, well, grasp, haha.

That's not to say that we use meditation as another weapon against ourselves to punish ourselves for not doing it right. "God, I've noticed I'm such a grasper. I'm so tense." Notice the layers. We get nice and still and notice and let go. We constantly let go. Continually bring our awareness to the places in our body where we feel that tension manifesting. Instead of recrimination or self-flagellation, we just let it go on the exhale.

This meditation is a step away from ignorance. I can't tell you or show you what you're ignorant of. A master can. Masters are like that. Buddha was a master and there are living masters today. But right now there is just you and I and these words on a screen or paper. What can we do to relieve ourselves of ignorance?

Practice.

Why You Suffer: Aversion

To avert means to avoid, dodge the bullet or run away from something that is undesirable. For many people, a moment where we are undistracted reveals that our underlying feelings are something to avoid. This is one reason we're so fragmented, distracted and addicted.

We need to develop the internal fortitude to face all moments, undistracted, and integrate our undistracted, pure awareness in all symbolic experiences. All experiences, incidentally, are symbolic.

My practice is about integration. In this view, it's not like Buddhism is one thing that's separate from posture based yoga, or that this meditation is legit and some other one isn't. We work with the total energy of our experience, which includes any teaching experiences that we encounter. From a *tantric* point of view, all experiences are teaching experiences.

This whole practice business really *is* about the state beyond concepts. There is no other point, no other aim, no practice that will get us there and nothing that we can elaborate upon. There's no framework. No foundation. There is no action that does not qualify as a vehicle for finding ourselves in that state. In this sense, we integrate with everything; space, air, water, fire, earth. So how do we do that?

To help us figure this out, I'll do my best to share my experiences, raw vulnerabilities and the reasons why we need to abandon *all* hope. You may or may not reject this "information." But as I told my boss, an Internet millionaire, Type-A, hyper intense individual on our four minute Uber ride to a fancy lunch, "The state of total relaxation is what's real. First, we relax. Then we create a vibration and manifest it outwardly from there. So let's learn to relax a little better. It's healthy and easier on those around us." He fired me not long after that. It's hard to talk real personal development to people like that.

We can try different practices to help us with this. But we shouldn't think that we always have to do the same ones in the same ways at the same times. We can learn to go beyond practice. But for most of us, that's a lot to ask. Miles Davis said that we first need to learn the rules (of jazz), then we forget them and play our guts out. Obviously, if we don't learn the rules then we're apt to spin our wheels or reinvent one that's already been done. Not necessary. Learn your meditation scales and mantra chord progressions and play it off the page (as a musician who reads music would) until you can improvise with your eyes closed, playing your heart out with no thought whatsoever. I don't know how long that will take. Most people don't pick up a horn and blast out Miles Davis' *Kind of Blue* on their first try. And most practitioners don't become Buddha the first time they sit still for a few minutes. In recovery, we say that time takes time. Good practice, then, takes practice.

So we begin in the space and time that we find ourselves in, and do our best. Remember to apply the principle: first learn the rules, use the tools, then transcend them. This is a life practice. Train yourself to remember this often, with every breath.

Meditation

Find stillness even if there are distractions in your environment. Approach the reading as a meditator. These are not just words on a page. Look for the real meaning with your deepest inner eye.

In terms of the way we'll enter into our meditation space, Longchenpa refers to it as the "spontaneous involvement." So we'll sit silently, looking to discover spontaneous involvement.

"How does this spontaneous involvement take place? This could be understood through nine analogies...like Indra, a drum, clouds, Bramha of the sun the most majestic wish fulfilling gem, an echo, space in the earth. For as long as conditioned existence endures, Buddhas insured benefit for others effortlessly and yogins are aware of this.

They manifest like the form of the lord of the gods reflected in a precious jewel. They offer excellent counsel like the drum of the gods. The sovereign lords amass clouds of supreme wisdom and love which pervade the realms of limitless beings up to the pinnacle of conditioned existence. Like Bramha not wavering from his untainted realm, they display emanations to the greatest existence in manifold ways. Like the sun, their timeless awareness radiates its brilliant illumination."

Let that one sink in.

"Like the sun, their timeless awareness radiates it's brilliant illumination."

How does it feel to consider timeless awareness? Imagine your awareness is brilliant, illuminating the way for infinite suffering beings to find their way out of pain, but not by rejecting it.

"Their enlightened mind is totally pure like a precious wish fulfilling gem. The enlightened speech of victorious ones, like an echo, is ultimately beyond words. Enlightened form is like space, pervasive without form and continuous. Like the earth, Buddhahood has served as the ground for all spiritual medicine without exception, which nurtures what is positive in beings."
-Longchenpa

Let those words resonate to a place beyond concepts. Live from that place. If that makes no sense in this moment, that's OK. We have plenty of experiences to try out. Return to Longchenpa's passage often. Find other quotes from enlightened masters. Keep a Dharma Swipe File of quotes. Swipe useful quotes whenever you can and add them to your file. I use Evernote so I can add, edit and access my notes from anywhere.

Meditation Asana

We have our *asana*, meditation position. There is no position which is not an asana. There's no position which is not a meditation position. But we artificially and superficially put ourselves into what we think is a meditation position. Then we give ourselves permission to meditate. Does that make sense? When you sit to meditate, assume a straight back. Be nice and still. Your eyes can be soft.

Simply notice. That is the extent of all teachings. That's the most that can be said. *Simply notice.* Remain in this position for five to thirty-five minutes at a time.

Eventually you won't need a special position or a cool shirt that looks like you bought it from a street vendor in Nepal to mediate. I don't know how long "eventually" means for you. Wear your shirt if you want to. Someday you may notice raw naked presence. What will you wear then?

All teachings are but elaborations on this point, to help us get into and remain in the real awareness of what can be called *Buddhamind.* This is the enlightened state of all Buddhas. This is our real state. But we refuse to see it. Does that statement bother you? It should. It should eat at you for the rest of your life, or the next seven or twenty-one lifetimes or more, until you become able to *know* that, *be* that and *never fall back* from that. All systems point to this state. Few will get you there and those that do might take forever. Best to be Present. Be aware. Be awake right now.

If we're not committed to this, it will never happen. This is why we meditate on death, suffering and so on. If we don't practice, we will struggle forever in samsara. The problem for us is that we don't want to awaken to reality. We reject it. We refuse to consider it, let alone acknowledge it and live in it. My teacher always says, in regard to our endless thoughts *about* practice, "That is a nice *idea.*" But ideas are insufficient. Enlightenment is not an intellectual process. When your mind hears that, it might say something like, "Haha, yes it is. In fact, enlightenment is my new project. Hold on, let me make a spreadsheet with a pivot table and a slide deck." However, charts and tables will not awaken you to a state of Buddhamind. Our minds really try to organize everything. But we really need to be able to live in presence right in the midst of things that don't make sense, like the violence in the world that surrounds us, or the way people drive or that our spouse won't put the cap back on the toothpaste.

To awaken is something that some Western non-dualist "teachers" like to talk about. Non-dual means there is no separation of a sense of self and the rest of the universe. These teachers enjoy sharing stories of their "awakening" experiences. In the Dharma it's considered major bad karma to speak of our spiritual skills. It's even worse—really, really bad in fact—to make up stories about our level of spiritual accomplishment. The best teacher, His Holiness Dalai Lama, says, "I'm just a simple monk." His students call him the Buddha Chenrezig. But does he go around with his egoic stories of insight? Nope. Humility is one of the qualities made stronger through awakening.

To be awakened is easier said than done. We do our best. It helps if we help each other out. That's called *sangha*, or spiritual community. We don't have to do it alone. We'll talk more about that as we go.

Samsara

The cycle of suffering is deep and endless. In the East, this is common knowledge. If you say to a Hindu or Buddhist, "Well you only live once!" they may look at you like you're mistaken because that's a Western notion. Our consciousness travels from body to body. Sometimes it gets stuck in a formless dimension, with no body. Buddhists talk about realms, of which there are six. Within each realm there are multiple levels. In brief, the realms are:

- Hell Realm; bad. Super-bad. You don't want to imagine how bad. Hideous tortures that make the worse *Saw* scenes pale in comparison. Screams so loud they ripple up the spines of beings in the dark, lifetimes later.

- Hungry Ghosts Realm; think about life in eternity as a crack addict. All you have is desire, but it can't ever be fulfilled. It looks like you can get what you want, but at the last moment, it only leads to disappointment.

- Animal Realm; you're a cow, in the slaughterhouse, trillions of times over. Then you're a monkey, in the science lab. Then you're a dog, in a fighting ring. This doesn't end.

- Human Realm; you're you, living here, now, with an opportunity to awaken. Hint, hint.

- Jealous God Realm; you think you're a bad-ass because you have some power, but your power runs out. It's like an eternal *Game of Thrones* that nobody ever wins. But the lust for power does not subside.

- God Realm; you're convinced that you've arrived at the Eternal Temple. You have solar systems of beings who worship you. But it's a scam, like some infomercial on infinite loop. The promise to be free of suffering never manifests.

Being a god isn't all it's cracked up to be. You realize this when you wind up in Human Form again and can't handle it when everything doesn't go your way—like some prima donna pop-star.

All of these realms are *karmic,* caused by karma. The realms are impermanent, and can be transcended by blessings of benevolent beings and our own practice, once we're human. Cockroaches, for example, don't have the option to be on a spiritual path. Some books say that these realms are imaginary, or that we can experience them while we're in human form. But the traditional Buddhist texts and the teachers who elaborate on them feel that these are actual states of being that our consciousness goes through. You can meditate on each of these to see for yourself. Buddha didn't ask you to believe anything. The Buddha isn't a snake-oil seller. The Buddha is really your pure, awakened non-self.

The Dharma asks us to have the guts to contemplate our own suffering instead of running away from it. That's the first level. After that we're asked to contemplate the suffering of others. First we consider the welfare of those closest to us. Then our friends, acquaintances, the nameless, faceless masses and lastly our worst enemies and the enemies of humanity.

Infinite beings, infinite sufferings. Think of all beings who have ever lived, are living and who will ever live in the future. Wish them to be free of suffering. Develop that aspiration. Then do what you can to help them. This is called the path of the Bodhisattva.

Do you want to step onto that path? Think well.

Journal Practice

- What would you possibly have to gain from contemplating the sufferings of yourself and others?

- What would you have to lose?

CHAPTER TWO

THE FIVE AGGREGATES

Never forget how swiftly this life will be over, like a flash of summer lightning or the wave of a hand. Now that you have the opportunity to practice dharma, do not waste a single moment on anything else.

-Dilgo Khyentse Rinpoche

The Five Aggregates are (roughly):

- Form, matter (earth, air, fire, water, space)
- Sensations (physical, based on external stimuli)
- Perception (internal feelings, emotions)
- Mental formations, karmic activity (ideas, instincts, trainings)
- Consciousness (eight types)

Form is emptiness; emptiness is exactly form. This is from the famous Heart Sutra. Everything looks like something but is really nothing. It exists but it also doesn't exist. We have sensations, like pain and pleasure. We feel things like happiness, sexual love, anger, depression, curiosity, empathy, disgust. All of our experiences are *impermanent*, they all come and go, but the karmic force of these experiences make them seem real, and as if they'll last forever. Samsara is very convincing. And if no one asks us to challenge the assumptions, we fall into all sorts of beliefs about everything. In the news as I was writing this, I read about a guy who tried to shoot up Google headquarters because he was upset that they were watching him. We perceive things through our senses and our minds and ascribe meaning to our perceptions. To that man I'm sure his experience that Google was watching him seemed very real. It's helpful to understand that perception and meaning can change with time, context and experience.

One day we're young and in love and it's us against the world and then twenty years later we can barely bring to mind the dim memory of our one true love's face. We formulate ideas, structures, organized sets of thoughts. If we put them on paper and convince enough people that these thoughts are true, well then we can have a religion, a state, a manifesto, constitution, school of thought, a holocaust or a great TV series. These aggregates are all connected and collected and fused and interwoven in ways that we can't see through or tease out unless we begin a serious meditation practice. Consciousness is like that.

The Buddha taught that there are five aspects of our experience that cause us to suffer. Why do they cause us to suffer? Because we think they're real. We fixate and obsess, even if we don't realize we're doing it. The five aggregates are connected to something called dependent arising. Dependent arising means that everything that comes into being does so because of a preceding cause. Every phenomena, thought, dream and feeling exists because of something that preceded it. We can meditate on the cause that preceded the cause that preceded the cause— ad infinitum. The point of this type of meditation is to realize that there is nothing that *really* exists, at least not in the way that we think it does. That includes our identity as well. Since nothing is as it appears, we are not as we appear, especially to ourselves.

There are many famous texts and entire schools that are devoted to just seeing the dependent arising (or dependent origination is it is also called) of all phenomena. Study Nagarjuna, for example.

Some people decide to go to a Buddhist college or make a life-time of study of this with Buddhist masters. Perhaps it's neces-sary to become a monk or a nun to really have the time to devote oneself to such levels of practice. See my book, *The Power of Vow* for more on that. I don't think it's necessary to become a monk. As *laypeople*, non-monastics, we can still work on our med-itation to gain awareness and understanding. We can still realize our Buddhanature.

We must learn to see dependent arising in ourselves. That's how we can gain nothing from Buddhist practice. It's like hearing a song that we've always known. We have an *actual experience* that is undeniable. In this experience we know in a way that is beyond the mind that *we are the space* in which all phenomena arise. We are, according to Dzogchen, the space and the infinite potential-ity, non-dual. It's not God doing it to us or for us. It's not some-one else's fault or problem. We are not solid or permanent. Yet the ego always convinces us that we are.

We might meditate for a while and think we know something about this. Be careful. New meditators often parrot the words of teachers and books. Sometimes we offer advice to friends and family. *I know you're mad at me, but remember, that's just your ego.* This is a perversion and distortion of the teachings and is the opposite of practice. If we're really able to reside in the calm state of not knowing, we won't react negatively to people, places and things. Remember, the fruit of practice is a life that works.

We can understand conceptually that the Five Aggregates are illusory. It's a fun idea to play with. The issue is that we energet-ically cling on a deep, fear-based internal level to the obsession that we are permanent, fixed beings. We might say that we're open and fluid, but are we? How open are we when it comes to money? Political values? Protecting our loved ones? How do we cling when someone we have helped is ungrateful or even causes us harm by lying about us? To bring our practice to fruition, we must let go completely, and remain free. This, as my teacher says, is not so easy.

The five aggregates and the phenomenal universe and our egos are not caused by a God or a creator or a universe either. That is a fantasy that we tell ourselves to feel better. The teachings of Buddha tell us that everything is created from its previous cause. But remember, Buddha doesn't ask us to believe anything. Try the Dharma for yourself and see what makes sense to you. In reality, there is no single cause. There are an infinite number of causes leading to any existing phenomena. Trying to trace the causes back to a source is impossible. Mathematicians and scientists use advanced formulas to try to source a single cause or set of causes of any event, such as a disease. Sometimes they get close and create some treatments that seem to slow down or eradicate some diseases or their symptoms. But how close do we get to eradicating the cause? To transcend mind completely, Buddhist practice asks us to become scientists of our own minds. Not true believers. Not preachers or marketers. Practitioners.

To do so we must accept what seems to be the impossible challenge, namely, to see that the Five Aggregates are compounded, illusory and impermanent. That means that they seem real. The floor we stand on seems real. Our ideas seem to be so good, so true. But everything from our dreams to our money to our deep clinging is like light shimmering on the water. Every moment our conception of identity is formulated by the transitory flow of thoughts, memories and sensations. We tend to get stuck in one frozen bubble of an idea on who we are. The Dharma tells us this isn't true and asks us to look into it. This can be quite alarming. To stay grounded as we walk the path, we need a stable practice with a group and a teacher that we can take refuge in on our journey.

There are so many causes, so many conditions. Yet our minds tend to isolate and stereotype and compartmentalize and pidgeon-hole. I recently met a cancer researcher. I said, "How close are we to finding a cure for cancer?" I didn't even realize how ignorant my question was until I listened to his extended answer. He said that there are hundreds of cancers with different variations. Some are more aggressive, some occur earlier, some later in life. With so many different types, isolating a cause is very difficult. In over a hundred years of research by the best minds with billions in funding and the most sophisticated labs all over the world, there is still no isolated single cause and no cure for cancer. There are many treatments and some are more effective than others for different people at different times based on the individual's system. Even the best treatments are not always 100% effective. Cancer often returns. I've lost several friends and family members to it so I've seen first hand how ambiguous treatment can be.

I'm in no way a medical professional. I'm just trying to make the point that we radically and drastically overgeneralize causes and conditions in our world view. We make a lot of assumptions all day every day. We have to, or we wouldn't make it from home to work and back. But we can't really point to one cause of anything in the universe with any serious degree of validity or predictability, especially our own experience. We don't even know what our next thought is going to be or what we're going to be doing two weeks from now or what we'll dream of tonight or in six months. This is because of dependent arising. There are simply too many variables causing a numberless amount of things to happen in the inner and outer universe. We can guess, but there is no way to know what will occur next because we don't really know what really, fully happened a few moments ago. It's impossible.

We can see that two planes hit the twin towers and thousands of people died. But fifteen years after 9/11, we still can't say with total certainty what happened. Whether it's an historical event in the world or a fight we had with our family member, our accounts are different from other's accounts and no one remembers it exactly the same. There are theories on how everything is traced back to a Big Bang. As the Dalai Lama has said, Big Bang, sure. But not just one Big Bang. He's also said that maybe consciousness created the brain, not the other way around. It's all guesswork. Nothing is certain. Our field of experience is fluid and ever-changing. But we tell lies to ourselves that it's all quite real and very important. Try insulting someone's favorite football team in their hometown bar and see what happens. Belief is incredibly strong. But it's not based in reality. None of it. Zero. It's all space, and a shimmering light show. But you'll never believe Buddha, let alone me. You'll have to take yourself down a path of meditation, if you have that interest, to find out for yourself if the Buddha was on to something or if he was out in left field.

Think about dependent origination as being the same for cancer or history as it is for your ego, your sense of who you are. If finding a single cause or set of causes of a disease is this hard, think of how much harder it is to trace the thoughts, impulses, images and memories that are within your consciousness for just a day, let alone a whole lifetime. Those are all subjective in your own internal experience. Imagine trying to meditate on the causes for an infinite number of past lives. This may be mind-boggling, but think of the skill required for meditators who achieve such results. Their histories and cases are documented throughout Buddhist literature, particularly in the Tibetan systems. I've listed some practices at the end of the chapter for you to work on to get a start on this type of meditation.

We can't be sure. Science can't be sure. So how can religions be sure? A religious person can be convinced of something. Some people are convinced that gays are somehow evil and should be killed. How does this make sense to that person? It doesn't make sense to most people. But to that individual, in their context and history, their karma brings them to that place. What caused that mass murder in Orlando in June of 2016? Was it hate? Islamo fascism? A bad upbringing or a chemical imbalance? From a conventional perspective, we can see how the media and our friends on Facebook jump to ridiculous conclusions. Nothing can be proven. There is always a shadow of a doubt because there can be no certainty about anything. But we tell ourselves and each other stories without rest. From a non-Buddhist view, the world just keeps spinning and God or the crazy people or the evil corporations caused it all. But from a Buddhist view, we must challenge *all* assumptions. It's a science of mind, requiring analysis of every aspect of existence.

Aggregates are called so because they're aggregated, or connected, or collected in such a manner that it's almost impossible to tell them apart. It seems that we are this one thing. But we're all of these things and, as crazy as it sounds, we're none of these things.

If we get really into meditation for a long time, we can notice the difference and sameness of all of the five aggregates. What's important to notice is their illusory nature. They're not real. They come and they go. But we somehow fixate on permanence. If we try to meditate on the body alone, we run into all of the aggregates. If we meditate on our energy by itself, we can't but notice the five aggregates. If we consider the mind as our object of meditation, the five aggregates will haunt every moment.

Sometimes I get feedback that readers feel somewhat alienated or unable to relate if I use terms like realization, enlightenment, non-duality or liberation. Perhaps you just want to feel a little better, get calm, be less stressed. I agree that all of these types of byproducts of meditation are great, but they're not the main point. I would be remiss in expressing the dharma in any way other than this main point, namely, that we all have the ability to awaken to our highest reality. In fact, any other goal is a distraction. Patanjali, the famous author of the Yoga Sutras, wrote that even magical powers attained in the process of practice are a trap for us. We must learn how to get in touch with our enlightened state, cultivate and nurture that realization like a mother nurtures an infant, and learn to keep from "falling back" into ignorance. That is the main point of any real teaching. Gain the knowledge which you already have, which you are already an expression of. It begins with the correct view. And in the Dharma, we can accept different views as correct if they help us in our practice. We just need to keep in mind that the views change, as they too are impermanent.

In, *The Five Aggregates: Understanding Theravada Psychology and Soteriology*, Mathieu Boisvert says that the five aggregates chain us to the "wheel of misery." He goes on to say that to identify with them is the wrong view. So it's through meditation of body, energy and mind that we can begin to see a crack in the mirror that will lead us, as my teacher says, to see the true nature of the mirror. In other words, our real nature. Different traditions will call this by hundreds of different names; the Higher Self, God, Universe, Elohim, The Lord, Christ Consciousness, The Light, Jehova and so on. But these are all wrong, from a Buddhist perspective.

The mistake is to personalize or identify with our real space, our true non-existent non-self. It's like the nature of a mirror. The mirror itself has nothing, no identity, no objective, no reflection. The mirror only has the potential to reflect. For it to do anything, we need light, an object to reflect, a seer to observe the reflection. I realize that to think this way will probably rock most people out of the water. Fowler talked about State Six in his *Stages of Faith* as, "exceedingly rare. The persons best described by it have generated faith compositions in which their sense of an ultimate environment is inclusive of all being. They have become "incarnaters" and actualizers of the spirit of an inclusive and fulfilled human community." Teachers, cult leaders and ego maniacs can in the hopeful eyes of the unwitting, seem to project these qualities. But, as Fowler later pointed out, they try to make the new world and the new faith in their own images.

So all of these gods and names for gods and naming of gods and projecting our human characteristics onto gods is just nonsense. No matter how powerful, grand, noble, jealous or kind any of these god projections are, they're still projections *onto* the mirror. Does that make sense?

The Twelve Links of Dependent Arising

1. Ignorance

2. Karmic activities

3. Consciousness

4. Mind and matter

5. Six sense-doors

6. Contact

7. Sensation

8. Craving

9. Clinging

10. Becoming

11. Birth

12. Old Age and Death

In the Twelve Links teachings, one cause depends on another to keep us in the unending samsaric spiral of suffering. We're ignorant of our real nature. That ignorance leads us to believe that we need to create an activity. The action is fueled with intention. We create karma like this, from the beginning. We remain stuck in a sort of dream-like conscious soup in which we think and create and feel and crave and act and regret and take in more data and continue to build layers upon infinite layers of delusion on top of our erroneous conclusions. We cling and we clutch. We create and we hate. We bring ourselves into being and we die holding on to our last thought. Unless someone teaches us how to live and how to die.

I recommend reading *The Tibetan Book of Living and Dying* and finding a fantastic teacher who will guide you through those teachings on the *bardo*, in-between states. The only way to break the infinite cycle of the twelve links of dependent origination is with powerful Dharma medicine, dispensed continuously from a teacher and a sangha, a community that believes nothing and questions everything. It's like spiritual anarchy. No thought is free of inquiry. No beliefs go unchecked.

Mirror Practice

Go stand in front of a mirror. Ask yourself who that is. Is that you? You know it's a reflection, but meditate on it. Is it real? You'll say no, of course you know it's not real, but honestly, look at your reaction. How do you feel about what you see in the mirror? Look closely. Look deeply with your feelings. Try this exercise in a room with no windows but a good mirror. Look at the projection of you. Turn off the light. What do you feel like? Turn the light back on. How do you feel now? Can you get a sense of the nature of the mirror as having no identity whatsoever? Then there's a picture of you that shows up. Can you consider that your nature and the nature of the mirror are non-dual? There is no identity, no name, nothing to name and no person to name anything. Just potential and things to reflect—space and our projections.

Lunch Practice

We can begin by meditating on what we had for lunch yesterday. Use your powers of meditative concentration to trace back your lunches as far back as you can go. If that's doable, try to trace back your feelings as far back from the present moment as you can. Then work with your thoughts.

Meditations on the Five Aggregates

In this type of meditation, we'll be trying to take a good, strong look at our experience. The way my old Zen teacher taught this was to *just notice*. That means we don't add anything, not even words. This is really the essence of Zen practice; just sit, just walk, just breathe. Your mind will attempt to do other things. Just notice that. If you can get into the just noticing state, you'll be in what is called Beginner's Mind. If you can just be in the just noticing, you'll be a very good practitioner. If you can stay there all of the time without ever being distracted, you'll be a Buddha.

Remember that our experience is aggregated, but not separated. It's all connected. We see-feel-think-are aware all the time. It's all happening simultaneously. Buddhists call this experience *compound*. So the lines between the five aggregates may be difficult to discern and are actually arbitrary since they're all happening in the same instant. This kind of practice is difficult but the results are profound. It takes a lot of skill to begin to notice what's happening in our human embodiment. Practice requires courage, patience, diligence and for most of us, lots of time.

The good news is that you can work on this practice for as little as 30 seconds at a time. Of course, if you have more time that would be great. But you can set yourself a reminder to go off on your phone once per hour. When the timer dings, pause for 30 seconds and notice one of the five aggregates. Then relax and go on about your business.

You could set this up to do one aggregate per week for five weeks. Or one per month. Or one a day. It's up to you. How do you want to practice?

Form, matter (earth, air, fire, water, space)

Notice the colors and shapes of your environment. Experience them for what they are, colors and shapes. Try to be aware of the difference between just noticing the raw elements and any sensations, emotions, thoughts or ideas about your universe. Treat each moment as if you just opened your eyes on this planet for the first time and found yourself without any context or frame of reference. This is an experience of being in the raw presence of the first aggregate.

Sensation (emotion, feeling)

Pause and notice your emotional experience in this moment. Don't worry about labeling it. In the first meditation we noticed externals, form and color. Here we notice our internal feelings. Did you ever have trouble answering if someone asked you how you feel? We've all seen those charts of 50 feelings with emojis for each. I'm not asking you to figure out how you feel. Buddha is asking you to feel how you feel, without concepts, without labels and most importantly, without judgements. It's especially challenging to notice the difference between a physical sensation that's occurring from an outside stimuli and some internal sensations. If you think about it, or rather, meditate on it, there is no such thing as external and internal. It's all a projection. But we have feelings and they tend to dominate us. So it's good to get a little space between "us" and our feelings by practicing a little five aggregate meditation on our feelings.

Perception

We have the five sensations and mind, so Buddhists talk about having six consciousnesses. Here we can meditate and observe without adding anything to the sense consciousnesses of sight, sound, taste, touch and smell. Think of this meditation as being conscious of each of the six senses separately. What do you see? Don't describe it, just see. Hear. Taste. Touch. Smell. You'll have ideas. You'll have feelings about your perceptions. They're inextricably linked. But try to relax in the state of just perceiving. This kind of practice can be extremely grounding when we're losing ourselves. Get good at it.

Mental formations (Karmic activity)

We have what are called mental events. Some of them are ideas. Some are filtering through stuff that matters from stuff that doesn't. Some are dreams. We can spend decades in therapy trying to sort out our mental formations. Or we can use Buddhist psychology and observe these as they form out of empty space, come into a state of appearing and then disappear.

Buddhists list these mental events out in extraordinary lists. You can find them in the texts. When there's nothing to do but meditate and keep the monastery clean, there's a lot of time for filing and categorizing mental events. Don't let that worry you. Just notice your ideas about your dimension. You have a lot of ideas, we all do. We have stuff programmed into our DNA, way beneath the surface of conscious awareness. We have our parental training, our social conditioning, or formal and informal education. We have our own ideas and the push and pull of karma from an infinite number of previous lives. So there's plenty of material in our karmic minds to work with. Somehow we must transcend it all and go beyond mental formations. This practice will help guide you in that direction. When you're sitting still for a moment, notice your idea and say mentally, "That's an idea," or, "That's a thought." That simple practice will bring clarity.

Consciousness

These may seem a little redundant. But the temptation to categorize and organize the mind is a little difficult. So we can try to be flexible about the overlaps. We actually have eight consciousnesses; visual, auditory, olfactory, gustatory, tactile, mental, emotional and global. We've more or less covered the first seven. So let's use our understanding of the fifth aggregate of consciousness to work with a global awareness. Take a moment to notice noticing. Notice with the "ground consciousness" that's like a dynamic awareness. Everything moves, comes into being and dissipates. A lot of things are conscious, subconscious and unconscious. In dream yoga, we can practice with the unconscious material and, if we meditate enough, that sub and unconscious material will arise in our "conscious" minds. Meditation itself can be some kind of bridge of awareness between these. Imagine if you could dream volitionally. Some people say they can. Tibetan dream yoga is a complete science of training in how to do just that. There are many books and teachings available on it.

Here, for our practice, let's just notice noticing. Global awareness that isn't fixed on one point, doesn't waver and doesn't change. This state of awareness is very deep and closely associated with a much higher state of Buddha consciousness. And, wait for it... it's already right here, right now. There's nowhere to go to find it. Find it.

Get real good at this.

CHAPTER THREE

THE THREE GATES

Body, Speech (Energy), Mind

*In naturally occurring timeless awareness, the ultimate heart
essence, there is no causality, so the abyss of samsara is crossed.
There is no better or worse, so samsara and nirvana are an
integrated mandala. There is no error or obscuration, so the
three planes of conditioned existence are seen though incisively.*

-Longchenpa

Teachers

As I discuss the Dharma, you may recognize some of the ideas that you've heard from different people. For example, if you're familiar with Eckhart Tolle, you may recall him speaking about "portals into now," which is an idea that I suspect he borrowed from the Dharma. Trust me, I'm a pretty open Buddhist, but a lot of Buddhists are hard core fundamentalists about their lineages. Many will only consider their own teachers to be legitimate sources of Dharma. These teachers and followers are quite limited. As I told a Zen teacher who had decades of sobriety and led many groups at the San Francisco Zen Center, "Your Zen is quite limited. My knowledge of the Dharma teaches us to go beyond limitations." Based on his expression, I might as well have been speaking Chinese.

While there can be value in any spiritual teaching, it's important not to plagiarize, repackage and rebrand authentic spiritual teachings. Some prolific authors are masters of this. They puts all teachings in charts and categories and tries to organize everything by some universal concept that they call things like Integral Theory. I would call this Mental Masturbation theory myself. It is interesting and useful but they don't always source their knowledge in the way that honors lineage. They repackages it as his own system, in my opinion.

Now, I do enjoy a good bit of intellectualization, but the mental path is still the path of mind. The intellectual analyzation and compartmentalization of Dharma is a trap. It leads nowhere. It doesn't lead to nothing, at least in the way we're talking about nothing. Nothing in our context here is the realization of nothingness. The experience of knowing is a place beyond words where *form is emptiness, emptiness exactly form*, from the Heart Sutra, begins to make sense. It leads to nothing in that you don't gain anything from the mental analysis except more concrete concepts. Does this sound like gibberish? It probably confuses the mind to hear these kinds of explanations. From a Dharma perspective, that's a good sign. So before you throw this book or your iPad against the wall, just try to understand that mental concepts are not realization. We can and to some degree must use some intellectual ideas to begin. But we can't get trapped there or stuck in that mental continuum. To become liberated, we must go beyond that. One path, or gate, or entry point is the body, which we will discuss shortly.

I'm a pretty big self-help fan. I learned a lot from listening and reading. There's a reason why some of these are international best selling authors and frankly, a lot more people listen to them than me or any Buddhist masters. But there are unbroken lineages of teachings for good reason. There have always been people who seem to borrow from the Dharma and try to sell it for themselves. What I do in my work is not some new program that is based on this or that but adds a new twist and adds value.

This book and everything else that I do is about my experiences and interpretations of real teachings from real masters in unbroken lineages.

There are unwritten laws against spiritual rebranding, and protectors in unseen realms who keep guard. Have you ever seen a Japanese temple where they have those massive statues of dudes with weapons outside the gate? It's something like that. We should be very careful with and respectful of authentic teachings.

Western non-dualists tend to refer to the Buddha's teachings as if they're something they came across in a recipe book. They like to compare, "It's like Buddha said," as if they understand what Buddha said. But it's not an intellectual process. That is the mistake that many people make in these days of instant online gratification. Someone hears something and repeats it and then it gets repeated and pasted onto an image that makes its way through social media channels. Pretty soon people go, "yeah, it's like Buddha said." Buddha might not have said that at all. That's why it's important to have real teachers who teach real Dharma and give you the best rundown that you can get to apply Dharma in our modern world.

Trust me, if you heard it on Twitter, it's probably bullshit. Having said that, there are some cool teachers that Tweet and I follow them. But please be discerning. I worked in the Personal Development field for a while and met many people who snagged any idea from any source and included it in their BONUS OFFERS BUY NOW CLICK HERE THIS ONE WON'T LAST marketing hype. Just be careful. Source your information. Don't be gullible. Trust your gut. Remember, to the

Personal Development Internet Marketers, content is meaning-less. They make their money off their pitches and they generally do not give one shit about you as a person, in my experience. There are always exceptions, of course.

That said, if we have our basis, our foundation (which we know is just symbolic) and we have some practice time under our belts, then when we see a Tweet or a meme, we can possibly have some way to interpret it in the context of actual Dharma. If we have a real Transmission, then we can understand that each moment, every experience—good or bad—is a teaching. Transmission is something that happens when we meet real gurus. They speak, transmit words, thoughts, energy, symbols, vibrations. We receive the Transmission and we have stepped on to the path. But most Westerners who don't follow real teachers think that if they hear one of these self-proclaimed Western Non-dualist pseudo teach-ers say something, that it's some kind of spiritual truth. But they really don't know what they don't know. Maybe in the long run it's not so bad, but the bottom line is we won't make much prog-ress without real teachings from an unbroken lineage by teachers who have realized the fruit of practice.

In order to understand teachings, we have to commit to them and practice for a long time and make sacrifices and put the prac-tice to the test. We don't just brush across teachings like some Facebook meme and act like we know something. But if we are committed, and we do practice for a long time, when we hear things by pseudo-teachers, dogs barking or airplane engines humming, we can understand the deeper meaning in which everything in the cosmos manifests. It depends on our karma and our view, our meditation and effort.

The sense is that any moment, any experience can be an opportunity for deeper awareness, until ultimately we experience absolute reality without distraction or "falling back," as Buddhists say. Remember, we can get glimpses, but to maintain a state of omnipresence is much more difficult.

A glimpse does not a teacher make.

I think I'm done digressing, but I can't be sure. Please continue reading with me though and I'll be sure to cover all of the points. I just want you to get a real sense of what Dharma is and be discriminating in what you take in. There's a lot of ego and a lot of hype out there.

Be Aware of Being Aware

In Buddhism, we talk about three dimensions, called The Three Gates. We'll discuss them generally before we get into specific practices for each. In the beginning of our practice, these are objects of our meditation. The object of our meditation is the thing we focus on. We can meditate on one, or more of these to develop our dynamic awareness. What do I mean by dynamic awareness? Awareness that stays stable while everything else changes is dynamic awareness.

Our normal level of awareness is scattered among many things. We're constantly distracted. When we get our Zen on, we first work with an *open awareness*, then engage in an *intentional awareness* which becomes a more *focused awareness*. You already know the feeling of focused awareness. It's like when you're deep into studying, watching a movie, making love, dancing or skiing down a hill. That sense of no separation between you and the action (skiing), or object of focus (your lover) is focused awareness. In this state, there's no separate "me" dancing, there's just the movement and the sound and the vibrations all integrated into a sense of oneness. When we're all up on our Zen like that, we're kind of oblivious to anything outside of our field of focus. That kind of concentration usually happens naturally, and often by accident, like when we're not really trying. But through meditation practice, you can learn to do it at will. I'll show you how.

Dynamic awareness, however, is *awareness that is aware of being aware*. Dynamic awareness is aware of what is moving, shifting and changing but dynamic awareness isn't being moved, shifted or changed. Does that make sense? The difference between a focused awareness and dynamic awareness is that dynamic awareness doesn't block out any experiences or see them as distractions. When we're in that Zen focus, there's just the one object or sensation and everything else is pushed out of our awareness. *Yogis* (meditators on the path) do a focus practice called *pratyahara* which is a withdrawing of the senses to focus on the internal landscape.

But dynamic awareness isn't focused on any one thing. It doesn't move with the flow of energy of the universe. Dynamic awareness is stable, no matter what changes internally, within your own mindset, externally, or anywhere in the entire universe for that matter. The universe is, incidentally, an expression of your own mind. But the pure nature of your mind is unchanging awareness.

Is it the same as dynamic awareness? Maybe. It's related, but on a higher level.

It's important to note that many meditation systems only focus on one of these aspects at a time. Hatha Yoga, for example, can be approached as *just* a physical practice because in our culture, we move into postures. But nothing could be further from the truth. Hatha Yoga is an energy practice that uses the body, but very much uses our energy and our mind. We may take yoga at the gym or YMCA and never know that the poses themselves are just the setup for the energy flow.

Zen meditation schools may focus just on breath or posture or mindful walking, though ultimately the practice of Zen becomes a non-dual experience of oneness. Vipassana or Insight Meditation systems focus primarily on body awareness without moving into different positions like yoga systems. It's done mostly in a seated posture.

We exist in all three dimensions simultaneously, so we can practice with that reality instead of pretending that one or the other aspect of our existence doesn't exist. However, it is simpler to approach them individually and many practices exist aside from those mentioned above. We have the freedom to know what the big picture of the Three Gates is and we can design our practices according to our situation.

The Three Gates are

- Body, *nirmanakaya (Sanskrit)*
- Speech/energy, *samboghakaya*
- Mind, *dharmakaya*

They're called gates because a gate is a "place" where you can enter. The body is a door. Our energy is a door and our mind can be an entry point for profound realization. It may seem contradictory that the teachings point to a no-self, yet there's a you that can go from here to there. Ultimately, on an absolute level, there is no "here" that is separate from any other "place." But symbolically, a different conscious state can be thought of as being another place. When we say, "I'm in a good place right now," we're referring to a state of mind.

Our conventional sense of self isn't real. From an enlightenment sense, as long as you believe that you're you, then you'll never get anywhere. Our dualistic position is that there's a me that's here, in this place, that isn't enlightened. That me wants to go to a there that is not here, where I will be enlightened. None of it is true. There is no you. There is no here. There is no there. Yet, we talk as if these identities and locations are true. The words are symbolic. The meaning is deeper than words can describe.

However, we have the freedom to discuss these things knowing they're not *absolutely* true. They're true in a relative sense (see Chapter Eight). But at least we're working to build the consideration that this sense of an "inherently existent I" is false. It's easy to intellectually agree that there is no I. You might say, "There is no I, there is only no-self. I am no-self. I do not really exist." But if you were able to apply that practice on a deep level, you might do something crazy like not go crazy when you hear Donald Trump talk. Traffic tickets are no issue for no-self.

There are many methods, such as *karma yoga*, selfless service or the bodhisattva path of the *Mahayana* (great vehicle) teachings that help us to dissolve a sense of I by acting as if the I is not in fact important at all—no matter how it protests. That's a hard path. There is no I. Just walking. There is no I. Just breathing. No me. Just sitting.

With this consideration, we can enter into the Dharma by stepping through one or more of these gates. We enter into realization through one or more gates. I like the term portals.

Change Practice

- Make a list of five things in your life that change, even though you may not notice them. Hint: your breath, heart rate, blood pressure and digestion change, but unless you're meditating, you probably don't notice, and even then, not directly.

- Now list five things that haven't changed. At all. What has not changed an iota in your entire life? List those five.

- Next, meditate on what has changed and what has not changed. See if you can get a sense of the dynamic awareness that we discussed in this chapter.

- Maybe there's a someone who is aware of what changes and what does not change. Who is that?

CHAPTER FOUR

BODY

Although the profound key points of body are many, rest freely and relaxed, in whatever way you feel comfortable. Everything is included in simply that.

- Padmasambhava

I don't stop when I'm tired. I stop when I'm done.

-Anonymous Internet Wisdom

Physical exercise is Zen. Runners know it. Cyclists live it. Have you ever watched a basketball game or played nine holes of golf as meditation? Movement, dance, yoga, standing, sitting, walking are all doorways to enlightenment.

The Buddha talked about Four Moments; eating, walking, sleeping and sitting. In fact, you can find Buddha statues in most of these positions. They represent the practice of mindfulness in all of our activities, or as we say in AA, "all of our affairs." To step into practice all you have to do is shift your perspective at *any* moment.

Yoga is Zen. Going poo poo is Zen. Going to sleep is Zen. Speaking with kindness is Zen. Reading Google news, not reacting to Facebook comments, making love, not making love. Zen.

As we begin to meditate, we can practice with these three dimensions of our existence; body, energy/speech, mind. The easiest and most obvious is the body or physical level. Our *primary* experience, that which is raw, direct, real, and the one we work with first, is on the gross level. People vary in how much body awareness they have. Some are very focused on how they look, but not so much how the body feels. We can be so obsessed with the externals that we actually ignore physical signals. Mindful body practice can help us reduce stress, love our bodies, and feel more calm. It can also help us to know when it's time to change some habits. The more practice that we do on the physical level, the deeper our connection to our physical well being.

Others don't focus on the body until they become very sick. When we have high levels of pain it consumes us, to the exclusion of all else. We may not think we have to practice without these painful situations. But when we find ourselves in them, it can be a very opportune moment to lean in to our experience, rather than running away from it.

Those of us who have been traumatized can be totally disconnected from our physical experience. Meditation on the body can open up pathways to healing that can not be activated through other methods, such as CBT (cognitive behavior therapy) or talk therapy. In fact there are entire systems and programs designed on the notion that somatic (body awareness) processes are very effective in healing trauma. I'm trained in some of these, including a program called Warriors at Ease, a yoga teacher training program which deals with helping military personnel who have PTSD (post traumatic stress disorder) through body awareness, meditation, and yoga. I'm also certified in Y12SR, Yoga for 12-Step Recovery which deals again with healing trauma in addicts and their families. I'd be happy to share my group format for these if you'd like to do one in your area. Email me.

Wherever we are in our level of attunement with our bodies, this gateway has everything to teach us. The physical path is deep and powerful. Even though we have three gates, the physical level of existence can be a complete path in itself. What do I mean by a *complete path?*

A complete path is one that leads to the utter cessation of suffering for all beings. There are schools that teach liberation for the sake of the individual alone. But the cessation of suffering for all beings in samsara is the goal of our liberation. It couldn't happen any other way. If we're liberated, we automatically want to help liberate others because we know our own non-separateness. A path which doesn't lead to total liberation for the entire cosmos of conscious beings is incomplete. The purpose of individual enlightenment is to totally and absolutely free all suffering beings from the six realms that we discussed earlier. Caveat: this is referred to as the Mahayana path, or Great Vehicle. Earlier fundamentalist strains of Buddhism disagree with this path, but their thinking was limited by focusing on just the individual.

Why do I say that? If we're only focused on our own struggle, that leaves the other billions of suffering beings outside our realm of consideration. When we consider all beings, we take a much wider focus. An action causes another action which causes another action in infinite succession. If we create actions with intentions for good, we create merit which continues in an infinite succession. One positive, loving action creates a positive chain reaction that never ends. A little later (Chapter Seven) we'll talk about what Buddhists call The Two Accumulations of Merit and Wisdom. We collect merit in the relative sense and gain profound knowledge that is a bridge between the Two Truths of the relative and absolute. Our practice is based on the assumption that good causes good. If we focus on our actions and intentions with the salvation of infinite beings in mind, we create oceans of positive merit for ourselves. If we focus just on one being, namely ourselves, we gain less merits and accumulate profound wisdom much more slowly. Slow and steady can win the race but it will take aeons, not just lifetimes, if we proceed by just focusing on ourselves.

Enlightenment means knowing the truth on the absolute level. And beyond knowing it, living it. That means we have the knowledge of emptiness (wisdom) and the heart of compassion. How could anyone have these things and not be automatically inspired to save all beings who suffer? My teacher says we should try to do our best to work without limitations. We should know that it's our dualistic vision that keeps us imprisoned. Dualistic vision means that we see ourselves as separate from the rest of the universe. On the Mahayana path, we work to loosen our grasp to the concept of an individual self by doing practices that are geared toward the benefit of all beings. It's a bigger view, with less limitations, hence the term *Mahayana*, Great Vehicle.

In our meditation, we first notice our material experience— the container that we inhabit. It is difficult to tame the mind enough to come into a deep awareness of the physical body. One approach, which may seem counter intuitive, would be to use a mental exercise called a *koan* in the Japanese Zen tradition.

Are you ready to get all Zen-like and contemplate some little mental puzzles that can't be answered mentally? Why ask a question that can't be answered? Well, that's a koan right there:

Ask yourself the question which cannot be answered in words.

Here are your instructions: sit with each of these questions until the answer for each arises from a wordless place. When that happens, confirm your mini-realization with a Master teacher. A Master teacher is not likely your 22 year old Core Power Yoga instructor. My opinion is to check with a real Master, tell them your realizations, and see if they buy your ideas. They'll know if you're intellectualizing or if you're experiencing a *siddhi*, attainment. An attainment in meditation manifests as the fruit of your meditation. These fruits can range from having less problems in daily life to magical powers such as clairvoyance. I say to find a Master and check with him or her because it's very easy for a Master to see all your karma, past lives, dreams, and future. They're impossible to bullshit. We can deceive ourselves so easily, so to have a real teacher is indispensable to obtain nothing from Buddhist practice.

However, if you are open enough and intuitive enough to receive, even your sophomore yoga teacher can trigger answers deep within you, even if they're unaware of it or quoting from a book. I've had a lot of accidental breakthroughs in classes like that. I read in a Zen book once that you can learn everything from a blade of grass.

When the yogi is ready, the simple can be profound.

Puzzles

If we pose the question, "Who's meditating?" We might spend considerable lifetimes looking for the answer, trying to discover the real meaning. If we "find our Zen," these questions dissolve. But then we lose our Zen and doubt arises. This cycle is called *samsara*. It only ends if we practice, which can take anywhere from an instant to a trillion lifetimes.

Does that mean we gain something from practice? Hint: that is a koan.

- Where is my body?

- Where does it begin?

- What are its boundaries?

- What part of my physical experience is the most real?

  - Pain

  - Pleasure

  - Numbness

- If I lost part of my body, where would my real body be?

- Am I my body? If my body were broken and doctors came up with a way to give me a new one, would I say yes?

- Who would inhabit the new body?

Meditation usually begins at the level of physical experience. It's the easiest gate to enter for some of us. We can notice the experience of the body and, as we observe it, we eventually come to some kind of insight. The insight that we come to is that the physical body doesn't really exist. This could happen instantly if we have the karma for it. Or it could take a very long time. It's hard to say. But we can begin.

When we first notice the body, the notion that it's not real might be hard to grasp. Try not to grasp it. Buddhists call this *non-grasping mind.* The body definitely doesn't exist the way we think it does.

I'll give you a personal example. I'm 54. I don't feel it. I'm married to a 25 year old, extremely fit yoga teacher. My body is very strong. We work out daily: take 6-7 yoga classes a week, indoor and outdoor rock climbing, weights, cardio, bootcamp classes, crossfit, swimming, skateboarding. I have deep depression several days a month. It gets bad in the afternoons. I get exhausted, then have to take a nap. When I wake up from my nap, I have horrible PTSD. I can't shake it. So I take my vitamins, go to a Bootcamp and a yoga class or some combination of a couple of hours of hard core workouts. Then I feel better. I've been like this for years and this system works one hundred percent of the time for me. So the body practice is very important in terms of workouts and fitness. But the meditation aspect of being still and working with the physical experience is equally important.

However, when I go to the gym, I look in the mirror and this is not the body that I think of. Not the one I'm used to. I can barely look at myself in the mirror sometimes. I want to know why there's fat around my waist and a belly that won't go away no matter how active I am. I want to avoid looking at the little wrinkles under my adam's apple. There is grey speckling my head and even on my chest. Ok so silver *is* the new black. But still, is this the body I had as a young man? Is this the me that I think I am? Where is the body of my twenties, when I ran, lifted weights, did martial arts, and rode my bike everywhere?

Despite the obvious evidence, my mind still somehow feeds the notions that:

- I am my body
- My body is as it's always been
- I can still do what I want with it

Of course, none of these are true. But *the push and pull of samsara* is quite convincing. To work deeply with the instability of our physical experience, we should meditate on the impermanence of the body and our eventual death. That's how the Tibetans meditate. The body isn't how we think it is. That's the first level of understanding. We can ask what it is in a reductionist manner (below) until we exhaust logic and reason. Most systems, however, start with a simpler meditation such as scanning the body.

Push Me, Pull You: Karmic Regression for Big People

As we proceed with our meditation practice on the body, we notice that there's a certain pull of the mind to pay attention to different things. This is the force of an infinite regression of *karma*. We haven't defined karma yet. It means cause and effect. Note: cause *and* effect. Which pretty much means everything. From the beginningless beginning of our conscious awareness, karmic seeds have been sewn with every action we've taken in any form or body we've inhabited. This karma has been fueled by our intentions and relative satisfaction (or disgust) that followed those actions. A karmic seed is a little potentiate that becomes an infinite chain of causality. These seeds can be purified so they never ripen. In a sense, this is the entire purpose of the Buddhist path.

For an action to create strong karma, three things are required. An intention, the action itself, and satisfaction. For every good deed that we do on purpose, enjoy doing and feel good about having done, we create merit, a cause for enlightenment.

Conversely, each time we do harmful things, in body, speech (energy) or mind, we build ourselves an impenetrable fortress of self-induced suffering. Karma happens on all levels; conscious, unconscious, thought, dream, intention, action. But to be heavy, we need those three things.

We can dig ourselves a karmic sinkhole with our selfishness, foolish desires, petty resentments, jealousies, fears. To be aware of this is incredibly demanding. It takes a tough individual to look at these things and strong resolve to work on them. We purify karma by letting go of its pull. We allow what *is* to *be*.

We apply this practice on the physical level by meditating on the state of the body. Fitness can be part of our meditation. Yoga class can be a strong support for our meditation. Walking mindfully can also serve this purpose.

In the Dharma, we talk about mindfulness. It's not some holy state. On the surface, it's just being aware and focused on one thing. But ultimately, our mindfulness practice brings brutal awareness of the suffering that we inflict on ourselves and others.

We also talk about vigilance. Every moment that we find ourselves distracted from our practice, be it from addiction or affliction or our deepest held conviction, we must return to our mindful practice. That's what Buddhist vigilance is all about.

This point is easy to understand intellectually. To apply it on an energetic level is an extraordinary achievement as a practitioner.

I just saw this in the news: A man ran into a guardrail in his SUV and climbed out as it dangled on a cliff. He stepped into the road and got hit by a tour bus. Karma. What does this say about his karma? So bad. But it was *his* karma. Every action piles up in the karma bank. We all pay our karmic debts. No one escapes. Well, unless we find the Dharma. The Dharma is the path to freedom from suffering. In a sense no matter how bad our karma is we can still find liberation. For some the path will be harder, that's all. We all want freedom from suffering. But what are we willing to give up to get there? Can we give up the outer, inner, and secret attachments and desires? Even the ones "no one" knows about?

We tend to think that our thoughts are private. No one will ever know. But the clairvoyants know. The energy feelers and medicine healers know. Our minds are like an ocean. Lama Yeshe said that. Consciousness exists in a vast, interconnected ocean. The yogis say that. Thoughts are causes. Causes have results. If we want different results, we must change the causes. There are different ways to change causes.

- We can crush them, block them, eliminate the negative ones and increase the positive causes.

- We can transform them into another manifestation of energy.

- We can allow them to dissipate with our non-grasping mind of pure, sky-like awareness.

When we change our karma to be positive instead of negative, we create merit. We need a lot of merit to find a teacher, and a path and eventually become enlightened. In this sense, we accumulate merit, so we can say that we do gain something from Buddhist practice. As we try to accumulate something, we have to train ourselves to let go of *everything*. But the deeper reality can't be added to or subtracted from.

Sounds fun, right?

Questions for Meditation (Koans)

- Who is it that inhabits this container?
- Who is the you that has this body?
- Where does desire come from?
- What happens to our thoughts?
- Why am I here?
- Why do I suffer?
- Why does happiness always end?
- Before you have an experience, where does it come from?
- After you have an experience, where does it go?

How do we meditate with a question? Doesn't that seem to be a mental exercise instead of a body meditation? Well, as I said, our body, energy, and mind are inseparable. But we can use the mind to meditate on the body and we can do a workout and a yoga class to clear the mind. We work with the different aspects individually but they're all interconnected.

The technique for meditation on a question is this: decide on one question, let yourself get still and quiet for a while, and allow yourself to bring up the question from a wordless place. Then you can non-answer it from a non-verbal space within you and thereby gain nothing from the practice. Every time your mind drifts off the question, bring it back. If it helps, put the question on a post-it note in front of you. Keep it burning in your subconscious 24/7 for a few weeks or months. These are suggestions. You'll have to find your own way to deal with the problem of koans. Teachers can't make it work for us. We have to come to the meditation space with the honest desire to practice. Then we have to put in the time and fuel it with commitment and good intentions. At some point, we just let go of all of it and relax into empty space.

If this discussion on Buddhist mental puzzles has blown your mind or confused you, don't worry. It's not the path for everyone. Following is a simple body meditation that you can do as your sole practice if you like. Or you can jump back and forth between these different kinds of practices. Do what makes you feel grounded, stable, clear, and awesome.

Meditation

Run your awareness from the soles of the feet, between the toes, all the way to the top of the brain, behind the ears and everywhere that you feel your body. In short, let your awareness travel around the physical aspect of who you are.

For some, this is the only meditation they will ever do. Many traditions would have you do it on retreats that last from days to years. Maybe you can become a monk or a nun and do nothing but meditate on your body for the rest of your life.

While you're meditating on the physical dimension, you could ask one of the questions such as, "What is my body? Where is the one place that is the body?" It's impossible to find. "If I lose a finger or a toe, am I less than this body?" I'm still embodied. I'm still *embodying*. Our awareness can flip back and forth like this. We can just begin to question, or have a sense of these questions as we explore our existence on the physical dimension. If these questions trouble you, you can just meditate on the five aggregates, all at once or one at a time. Find the gate that works for you.

When you try not to move and just relax in this physical space, awareness begins to awaken. You may feel invigorated, you may feel excited, you may feel depressed or sad—any range of emotions. The key in this type of practice is to be aware of spontaneous experience, the experience coming up out of nowhere, out of nothing.

Journal for post-meditation

- How do you find *your* Zen?
- What do you hope to gain from practice?
- How can being physical be your meditation?
- What forms of physical meditation can you commit to for the next few months, or a year.

We may like or dislike any aspect of our physical experience. If we're sick, it's very difficult to accept our condition. My old teacher, Joko Beck, used to say that the sickest people have the greatest opportunity. When we're faced with debilitating illness, we may finally face the inevitable fact that there's really nowhere to run. So the first gate or dimension of our experience is the physical, called the Nirmanakaya. This is the level on which Buddhas manifest the physical appearance, miraculously and spontaneously arising out nothingness. That's you and me right now, manifesting out of nothingness. You can just check it, notice this, notice what you're trying to change, notice what you're willing to accept and just notice the play between the two.

If you can practice that, then you're on the spiritual path. And if you discover that you are indeed on the spiritual path, not some bullshit path but a real one, then I feel bad for you. Because it's not easy. In fact, it's ridiculous.

"My advice to you is not to undertake the spiritual path. It is too difficult, too long, and is too demanding. I suggest you ask for your money back, and go home. This is not a picnic. It is really going to ask everything of you. So, it is best not to begin. However, if you do begin, it is best to finish."
-Chögyam Trungpa Rinpoche

As I've said before, once you're on that dang ol' path, there ain't no gettin' off it. Joko Beck used to say that once you commit to your meditation cushion, you can try to abandon it, but you'll always be back. It is like that.

CHAPTER FIVE

ENERGY

Although there are many key points of speech, such as controlling the breath and reciting mantras, stop speaking and rest like a mute. Everything is included in simply that.

- Padmasambhava

Body: Physical Energy

We have our physical energy that's related to how much stamina, strength, and vitality we have in our physical body. These types of energy aren't really separate, but we can talk about them to get an idea of how they function. When our energy in one area, say emotions, is out of alignment, it causes depletion in our body. Healing can happen on all levels with energy practices such as those found in Chinese Medicine, acupuncture, Taoism, Japanese Reiki, Shamanism (in over 60 different cultures), as well as Tibetan systems like Medicine Buddha, Yantra Yoga, and Moxibustion.

There are amazing teachers and instructions readily available on all of these energy healing practices. Some are passive, like Reiki and acupuncture, where you just receive treatment, but others are active like Taoist Qigong and Tibetan Yantra Yoga where you move and work with your energy.

Speech: Sexual Energy, Emotions, Vital Energy, Breath

Everything in our energy system is linked with our breath. When we work with our breathing as a meditation practice, Buddhist systems can be integrated with Yoga systems to bring benefit to our condition as energy beings. Caution: these practices may make you feel sexy. If you're looking for a way to repress your sexuality, this kind of practice may not be for you.

Sexual energy isn't something that you hear a lot about in typical Buddhist books and teachings. But it is a powerful aspect of who we are and is dealt with in secret tantras. This aspect of our human dimension is dealt with in Tibetan Vajrayana, Taoist Qigong, and various styles of Hatha Yoga. There are ways to maximize sexual energy and balance out our vital energies. The trick is to do so without getting attached.

Our emotions are linked with our energy, which is connected to our breath. If we control our breath, we can control our emotions.

When we practice sincerely for decades, the depth of our attachment becomes excruciatingly clear. With life experience comes loss. Some of us don't have to wait until we get older to lose a lot. But the older I've become, the more loved ones and possessions I lose. My mother died in '96, my dad two years later, my brother two years after that. My best friend died of lung cancer in 2001. Many people in the recovery community that I've belonged to since 1984 have relapsed and died directly or indirectly from drugs or alcohol. My young friend Tiffany was shot in the head by tweakers one night a few years ago. In 2014-15, I lost a 17 year relationship with my partner, almost all of my possessions and my best dog ever, who died in front of me of heart failure. There are more that I could list but you get the point. All of this loss brings a certain sort of sad wisdom. With the sorrow of letting go, we can find a practice much deeper than we ever knew before. This is my experience. Why is this relevant to our discussion on energy?

The reason is that not all Buddhist systems acknowledge energy. If they don't acknowledge it, how can they teach us how to work with it? We should know that there are different systems and understand the variants between them. Teachers tend to give their tunnel vision view from their own tradition or, as in the case of what I call Western Non-Dualists (or New Age Spiritualists), with no tradition. The new school teachers tend to speak from their own experience, like I do, but without a succession of teachers. Some quote Jesus, but in a mystical way, or claim to be channeling him, still others claim inspiration from, "God, Spirit, The Universe or whatever words you want to use." When people have a Divine Calling, be skeptical!

There are similarities in different spiritual teachings, but the point of view can vary widely. I had a friend who practices in the same system as I do, but he makes claims that various Hindu terms mean exactly the same thing as Tibetan Buddhist terms. But they do not. And different Buddhist schools and systems deal with the same terms and concepts quite differently. The point of view of Buddhism and its variants is unique, in that it puts the onus of responsibility on the practitioner and the practitioner alone. There is no creator god in Buddhism.

Since the POV (point of view) is different, that means the practices are also different. For example, if the main focus of a teaching is Presence, or self-restraint of character defects, we're not going to hear much about energy channels. We're not likely to receive instruction on squeezing our sphincters and pulling our chakra energy up from our butthole to the top of our head in an effort to practice ejecting our consciousness at the time of death.

However, we are energetic beings.

When we work against our own ethics or allow ourselves to be victimized by our own afflictions, addictions and ethical contradictions, it messes up our energy. Tantra is an energy path. It's called Vajrayana in Tibetan Buddhism. This is related to the Speech section in Body, Speech (energy), and Mind. Our practice with deities, such as Green Tara or Kalachakra in Vajrayana is about energy.

The tantric, or Vajrayana path involves having a guru. Not just any old monk, but a tantric guru or Vajra Master who has realized the fruits of the practices. He or she (mostly he but that's changing) gives a special ritual where the disciple is conferred an entry to the path, called an initiation. Sometimes these are done formally, especially with large groups, and at other times informally. In Tibetan Buddhism, teachers are called Lamas or "high ones." They generally have a lot of powerful energy and oftentimes the sangha that follow them struggle with infighting. I've experienced this first hand. If you do, just note that it's bound to happen that on the fast track to enlightenment that people's stuff will come to the surface. Dealing with it *is* the path.

When we enter such a path, it's best to check up and do our research ahead of time. Watch the students, see how they act. I'd apply this to a Vajrayana initiation, a yoga class, or a Tony Robbins seminar equally. But with the Vajra Master, we're said to be bound until enlightenment. So it is best to be sure. You can walk away from Deepak, but your link with the vajra master and family is a marathon to enlightenment, not a fifty yard dash.

The Vajrayana path is quick. We can attain nothing (liberation) in twenty one, seven, or even one single lifetime, as opposed to trillions of lifetimes in the Theravadin (sutra-based), mindfulness-only, or other more renunciate oriented paths of Buddhism. The path of the diamond vehicle is fast, and tricky. We can easily lose our way. We have to fine tune our mindfulness so we can detect our energy at very subtle levels. We have to know how to practice renunciation most of the time, and transformation some of the time. The level of intention, for example, can create a wave of energy that ripples through our karmic existence. Impure intention can set our dimension on fire. We can attain a ton of merit, then blow it up in a moment of anger. So we have to be very, very skillful practitioners to engage in the Tantric\ Energy paths.

Even if they appear to just work on the physical level, our Western styles of yoga practice, such as Hatha, Vinyasa, Ashtanga, and Kundalini are all energy related. Yet we have few, if any, living Masters in the West to guide us and keep us safe on this treacherous path. My yoga is rooted in my Zen and in my Tibetan training. So when I approach Hot Vinyasa for example, it's with the attitude of a seasoned practitioner. Even though I know how to practice, my road has been problematic. Stuff comes to the surface.

I began Zen training in 1991 and stuck with it pretty consistently. Throughout that time I was depressed but pretty stable, occasional angry outbursts notwithstanding. I entered into the

Vajrayana path in 2005. Things started getting dicey around then, but I didn't recognize it for what it was. I spent time with a lot of high lamas and highly charged, even crazy sanghas. I had high expectations of all of them. We didn't have any teachings like this in the Zen tradition, which I'd studied for over 15 years. I learned a ton from the Tibetans. I went to retreats out of state and abroad, and did many of my own home retreats. I hosted lamas, teachings, and study groups at my house. I took initiation after initiation in the four main Tibetan schools of Nyingma, Kagyu, Gelukpa and Sakya as well as in the Bon tradition.

I started taking yoga seriously in 2010. I took a heated yoga class every day and worked out at the gym and rode my bike. I became a yoga and fitness teacher and taught 15 classes per week for about five years. When I added all of that yoga and fitness to my practice regimen, all hell broke loose.

My sexual energy went from being totally flatline to over the top. The next five years, I had the most sexual energy in my life - even more than my teens and 20's. I probably had more partners in that time frame than I'd had in my entire life leading up to that point.

I went from Portland to a retreat in LA and inquired about this sudden upsurge in sexual energy with a long-term yoga teacher who has studied with my own teacher for over thirty years. He said, "Well that's to be expected, isn't it?" I didn't know that! I didn't expect it nor did I have any idea how to tone it down.

I thought I might have been addicted for a little while there and went so far as to check out some literature and meetings on the topic of sex addiction. That turned out not to be the case. I really just had a crazy libido from all of that energy stimulation.

The way that we can begin to explore this aspect of energy is to notice, simply acknowledge, be aware of the breath. The breath is linked with our energy. Our energy is our *prana* or vital life force. Prana can come in to us from any number of portals in and around the physical body, but the majority happens through our breathing. As newbie yogis, (remember, a yogi is anyone who takes the meditation path seriously) we need to breath the prana in through our airways. But advanced practitioners are said to have the skills to exchange energy directly with the five elements without taking in any food, water, or even air.

There are secret tantras (which require initiation and instruction from a qualified master) that describe these skills and how to acquire them. There are also accounts in places like Tibet of yogis who have been found meditating in an apparent frozen state in sealed caves, still alive after many years. Since we're just beginners, we'll set the bar a little lower at the beginning. But it is useful and interesting to know that there are stages that the watered-down mindfulness books and "teachers" don't talk about.

Mind: Mental Energy

Mind energy takes up a lot of our time. As a recovering alcoholic, the mental landscape can be a rough neighborhood for me to hang out in. We have a tendency to be plagued with obsessive minds. You may or may not relate. But as I've written in other places, Buddha would say that we all have addicted minds.

To the extent that we identify with ourselves as a concrete, inherently self-existent being, we suffer. We expend energy with every thought and we need brain energy to think clearly, solve problems, be creative, make plans, and remember things. If we're physically lethargic, we feel mentally dull. When we take our vitamins, do vigorous exercise, or meditate quietly, our mental energy becomes free and capable of being focused. It takes more mental energy to hold anger and resentment than it does to be in a space of compassion. When we opt out of anger, we walk away feeling lighter. If we're chronic worriers, we will remain in a state of ongoing stress and anxiety. All of this negative thinking, whether it's being a victim, obsessing over outcomes, or just being a non-stop hyper thinker, can deplete our mental resources. Meditation not only puts us back on track but after it gets ingrained in us, we tend to see the mental stresses emerging and dissipate them before they dig us into a hole.

When we work with our meditation on the Five Aggregates as we discussed in the last chapter, we directly address our mind state. Our mind state is the state of the five aggregates and the eight consciousnesses. Our real state is the state of the *vajra*, indestructible diamond essence.

The spontaneous engagement that occurs during our meditation (and eventually our post-meditation) is this awareness of manifestation (in this case the breath) as it occurs moment-by-moment. In the practice of real awareness, we're liberated from the experience, but we remain aware of the experience. We're immersed and integrated in the experience without being sucked into the karmic black hole (samsara).

Journal Practice

These journal questions are designed to help you see your emotional energy around the desire to fix what appears to be broken. I think most of us live in a state of perpetual dissatisfaction about our lives. When we meditate on the feelings in the body, it can have the effect of opening up energy channels. Think of it like a mental acupuncture session. In a sense, our penetrating meditative self-inquiry pierces holes in the veil of self-delusion. Remember that when we do this kind of work, we can sometimes get overwhelmed with the experience. So be sure to have your support systems in place. In the next chapter, I'll talk about one of the Buddhist support systems, the *sangha*.

- What are the three main areas of your life that you want to fix?

- What specific situations do you tend to want control over?

- Where does your tendency to correct and repair arise from?

  - Write about a time in your life that impacted your role as a fixer.

- How do you feel when you try to let things be as they are?

  - Describe those feelings in terms of physical sensations.

  - What is the energy like?

  - What thoughts accompany those feelings?

Meditation

In our first level of meditation on the breath, the level of Awareness, we're not changing the breath, or the physical posture.

We just notice inhalation and exhalation. Explore the following: as you exhale, notice that space of emptiness before you inhale. We're not trying to extend it yet or do anything different than notice how we breathe. But, we can notice immediately that we have a tendency to want to alter, modify, fix. It's important to notice and be deeply aware of our desire and tendency to correct, fix, repair, and improve. It will be helpful for you to explore this as you proceed with your practice on an energetic level.

Notice the breath, in and out. Where is the breath? I struggled with this for years. Where is the breath? What am I supposed to notice? Is it the nose, is it the belly, is it the lung? *I don't know where I'm supposed to be looking.* Inhale and exhale, notice that experience. Be non-dual with the breath.

Pranayama Practice: Simple Ujaii

This is an energy practice. In this practice, we shift from simply observing the breath to directing the breath. When we learn to direct the breath, we can learn to direct our energy and our emotions. There are many pranayama, directed breathing practices. Some are gentler, some more forceful. This one's easy, and very effective. Learn it.

Sit in a comfortable, seated position. Use a chair, edge of the bed, cross legged or half cross legged or with legs folded under you. Lift your heart. Shoulders up and back and down. Back of the neck long. Exhale. Relax. Breathe in deeply, exhale slowly. Draw the belly in on the exhale. Pause empty of breath. Constrict the back of the throat slightly as you inhale. At the top of the inhale, expand the lungs and gently breathe in a little deeper. Expand

and hold just a little, with your throat relaxed. No pressure in the back of the throat here. Gently exhale through a relaxed throat about one quarter to one third of your breath. Then constrict the throat again until you're almost empty of breath. Relax the throat. Exhale completely. Pause empty. Breath in a little through an open, relaxed throat. Constrict the throat a little until you're almost filled up. Fill up and hold. Repeat this breathing practice.

Do it often. Maybe consider taking a yoga class where they teach this during movement and postures. Otherwise, try it while you're taking a walk, going to sleep, sitting at your desk. Probably not while driving. But if you get pulled over, you might do it while waiting for the officer to speak to you. This is a good one to use to stay calm.

This is what I do constantly. Helps me when that PTSD hits.

CHAPTER SIX

MIND

Although the many key points of mind involve concentrating, relaxing, projecting, absorbing, focusing inward and so on, everything is included in resting in genuine simplicity, free and easy, in your own nature.

- Padmasambhava

The third gate or dimension of our existence is the mind. The mind is very tricky. It tells us things that are not true. In fact, from a Buddhist perspective, the mind can not tell us anything that is ultimately true. Not on the absolute level. In samsara, everything is relative. Knowledge of and the capacity to get in and stay in the state of awareness of the absolute is the only way out of the cycle of suffering, but paths vary on the methods used to get in that state.

When I first began to practice in the late 80's, I definitely wanted to gain something. I didn't know what. But I knew there was something that I'd get out of it. Otherwise, why practice at all? I wanted to fix everything. I felt broken. I knew in my bones that I was fundamentally flawed. At least that's how I felt. I didn't really know the truth, but I believed the smokescreen of appearances that my mind projected. It wasn't until 2005 or so that I really got a taste of seeing the nature of mind, instead of the projections of mind. At that time, in my first teaching ever with a Tibetan Buddhist nun, I understood that I was not flawed. It was enough to keep me going but not enough to stop the flow of mental karma. I've fallen back into the belief that I'm broken a million times since then. But I've never lost that knowledge deep inside me. That has been nurtured and developed with years of serious practice.

When I teach meditation, I always say, "Let the thoughts float by like clouds in the sky." When we practice like that, the mind responds. On some unconscious level, it sends messages like,

- Oh, but I like that one.

- I wish to develop that thought.

- I am quite intelligent.

- I appreciate the creative aspect of that, thought.

- Oh, that's very interesting.

- I would like to follow that thought and make it better.

The mind builds on thoughts and creates a fortress, an empire, a universe. But we can and must challenge our thinking. Notice the thoughts floating by like thoughts in the sky.

We may ask ourselves from where does this thought arise and where did it disappear?

This is already too much, this meditation is already beyond the capacity for most.

In this aspect, we just examine the flow of thoughts. Eventually we'll be in a space to simultaneously and spontaneously acknowledge the three aspects of our experience; the physical dimension, the energetic dimension related to our breath and emotional experience and of course, our mental experience. But we can make a start by watching our thoughts without getting hooked. Even after years of practice, I sometimes return to this one simple practice that was given to me over 25 years ago by my first Zen teacher: just notice thoughts.

The difficulty is to be able to observe the mind without changing anything. Don't change anything and don't try to *not* change anything. Don't push against it. Notice yourself not wanting to push against it. Our practice with the mind is about *just being* in pure awareness. Other practice is about directing the activities of the body, breath, and mind. We can do any and all of these practices or just one. But don't let the choices and freedom stop you from being a practitioner. They're all legit. Which aspect should you focus on? You are the only person who can answer that. Buddha wouldn't tell you what you need to do. He described the situation and gave a path out of suffering. But Buddha couldn't make you enlightened. You have to take responsibility. Practice. Practice well.

The layers are deep. The practice is deep. Your mind may not be ready for it. Your ego probably doesn't want to do it. We say we want to be Buddhists, or that we want to be in recovery, to be on a spiritual path. Well, this practice is it. Acceptance of our condition, noticing, acknowledging, being aware of it is our first level of practice. First we try to be aware of our condition before we try to accept anything. Just notice it.

I don't know about you, but for me this type of practice is really hard. We're not even paying attention because we're intensely distracted 24/7. We're so distracted we don't know how distracted we are. We're looking for a fix, we're looking for a change. So we might do this kind of practice where we just sit and notice one of these aspects for 10 or 20 years. We might go to a vipassana meditation program and just look at the physical dimension. We might enter into another type of system which acknowledges energy completely differently. We might go the intellectual route. None of them work. None of them help us to gain anything. But we can begin. That's kind of a koan isn't it? Why would we do anything if we weren't going to get anything out of it? Our problem, from Buddha's perspective, is that we think we need to gain something.

If we're hypnotized by the world of appearances, it's easy to think we have to get more, do more, be more. It's not just the media or the culture or advertising or the greedy corporations. They all exist to fulfill the demand that we supply. When we begin to examine our situation, we might find that the closer we look, the less substance there is. There's nothing to gain, and therefore nothing to lose. But until we experience that insight, trying to "get nothing" will just seem like an interesting idea if we're inclined to the Dharma or merely mental masturbation if we're not.

Three Ways to take Refuge

Remember earlier that we talked about the three roots of suffering:

- Attachment; sticking like glue to thoughts, ideas, experiences, desires, outcomes.

- Ignorance; having no idea that this process rules us.

- Aversion; pushing away the things that don't enhance our attachment. We can also be attached to aversion.

If we just looked at our attachments, we'd be doing amazing Dharma work. Eventually we might realize that we've been unaware of the situation of samsara this whole time. We might even stop resisting so much. This would be good spiritual work.

But some of us need a replacement for our normal activity cultivating, establishing, nourishing, and supporting the karmic delusion of the three roots. We can take some spiritual actions that help us create a new idea of who we are, or at least who we aren't.

Spiritual Identity

Just who do you think you are anyways? That's a question that a Buddhist teacher might ask, though maybe they'd say it nicer. So far our koans, journal questions, meditations and breathing practices have all been geared towards getting you some taste of practice. The hidden agenda or secret marketing tactic is to poke a hole in your sense of self. Hey, don't be mad at me. I didn't make this stuff up. It's really the whole purpose of Dharma. Be empty. Know you're empty, like space. There is no you. There never was. It's all like sunlight shimmering on the ocean waves. Temporary, illusory, and unreal. Just like a dream.

If you listen to the modern legends of self-help spirituality—you know, the ones Oprah hangs out with—you'll hear this teaching. Modern psychotherapy focuses on constructing, rebuilding, or at least coping with our useful sense of self so we can continue to pay into the social security system and our health plan and pay taxes and buy more things and, well you get it. But the Dharma does the opposite of psychological capitalism. The Dharma wants you to be more of a spiritual socialist. Work for the common good. Spread the wealth (of knowledge). That sort of thing.

AA taught me the same. Turn your will and your life over to the care of God as you understand Him. Him. Is He really a he? No idea. But that's what they say. Spiritual surrender. God's will. Higher purpose. Love and service. These are all spiritual principles of 12-Step programs. The main premise of the programs is that we're self-absorbed narcissists with a spiritual malady and we need to focus our lives on helping others in order to stay alive, grow spiritually, oh and, stay sober from our booze, people, substances or whatever. Buddhism asks the same, but in different ways. All the good spiritual systems that I'm familiar with are based on this idea that we're connected to a higher reality than what appears before us. In my opinion, Buddhist practice does the best job of giving us tools for exploration and explanations of the situation. You know, to relieve our spiritual constipation. Because we're basically full of shit when it comes to who we think we are.

The mind does all the thinking.

Refuge

I wrote a whole book about taking refuge vows and what that means, (*The Power of Vow*, 2013). The topic can get quite complicated. But here we'll go into this in a real simple way. The Buddha has some knowledge. He knows what's up. We suffer. The Four Noble Truths tell us:

- Life is suffering.

- Suffering has a cause.

- The cause can be eradicated.

- There is a pathway and system (more than one actually) to eradicate suffering.

Puritanical Buddhists will argue with the way I've presented this here, but this is my understanding based on my experience and practice. So we have this problem, life is suffering. And we have ways to deal with it. The first way to deal with it is to understand that we already worship our own egos. We're already addicted to our own attachments. When we think we're right, nobody can convince us otherwise. We hold on to things that don't help us like they used to. So we already hide out in our own mental bomb shelter. In that sense, we know very well how to take refuge.

To take refuge means to seek safety, shelter from the storm. The old Japanese warriors who defected from the battlefields sought refuge in monasteries. Maybe they didn't know that the real refuge wasn't behind the walls of the monastery. The real refuge is an inside job. And the good news is that we already have the capacity and mental faculty to take refuge. All we really need to do is change the focus. For that, we'll need a new object of refuge. Buddhism offers three.

The meditation on the mind is to direct the mind to a higher state by taking mental refuge. Here, we will use our minds, our words and our bodies to take refuge. Put your palms together with the sincere desire to find a higher truth. Then we say the refuge out loud. This is an integration practice of body, speech (energy), and mind.

The Three Jewels

The Buddha

The Buddha is the source of wisdom. He is a totally enlightened being. He can be trusted. His words, his teachings, his energy are a source of refuge for all suffering beings. We can simply declare our refuge by saying, "I take refuge in the Buddha," three times, out loud, in front of a group of Buddhists. Or one teacher. Or a statue of the Buddha. Or alone on the highway. There are no limits. You can take refuge in your own heart by sensing your body meditation, breathing your energy meditation, and concentrating your mind meditation on the flowing, interdependent, illusory nature of samsara. As you do so, question everything. That's good refuge right there.

The Dharma

The Dharma is the higher teaching. Remember that in Buddhism, we have many levels of Dharma. With our hands together, we say, "I take refuge in the Dharma," three times out loud.

- Hinayana, Small Vehicle
    - Restrain body, speech, and mind and meditate quietly.
    - Live a sheltered life.
    - Don't cause drama.
- Mahayana, Great Vehicle

- All of the Hinayana plus work for the benefit of all beings.

- Zen is a Mahayana teaching and practice.

- The Bodhisattva Path is Mahayana. This is the path of dedicated action to all beings even to the point of self-sacrifice.

- Vajrayana, Diamond Vehicle

  - All of the Hinayana and Mahayana, plus mantras (words), mudras (gestures), and visualizations.

  - Within the Vajrayana are:

    - Three Outer; Lower Vehicles

    - Three Higher Vehicles; Inner, Secret, Most Secret

The list above is a very superficial outline. There are literally thousands of texts in many languages and cultures that outlines these systems. I just want you to know that there are different systems and paths within those systems that you can study and practice and take refuge in. We can take refuge in any of these Dharma teachings by reading, learning, meditating, and living the principles of love and service.

The Sangha

The Sangha is the spiritual community of practitioners that one practices with. We can see the sangha as small as a few members, or as the group of living practitioners worldwide, or even the Noble Arya Sangha, the formless beings who have transcended the limitations of samsara by becoming realized beings. Whatever scale you use to look at taking refuge in the Sangha, the practice is to turn to the Sangha for support, inspiration, guidance, and friendship. Palms together, "I take refuge in the Sangha," three times.

It's important to understand that we need to take refuge with our body, with our breath energy, and with our minds. It's not just an intellectual or a devotional activity. In AA we say, "Every day is a day when we must carry the vision of God's will into all of our activities." In a Buddhist sense, we practice to live in an ongoing state of refuge. But there is the difficulty of being unable to see the Buddha, hear the Dharma, or spend time with the Sangha every moment.

It's more about what we don't take refuge in. We can choose not to take refuge in things like

- Fear

- Hatred

- Self-loathing

- Depression

- Anxiety

- The news

- Politics

- Being a victim

- Drugs

- Alcohol

- Vaping

- Sex

By choosing to bring our meditation practice into the body, we gain nothing from Buddhist practice. By taking refuge in the prana that our breath brings, we gain nothing from Buddhist practice. Then we can take refuge in thoughts of kindness, love, and compassion, instead of the ongoing demons of the mind. This is a good way to take refuge.

Meditation

All of the meditations that we've done so far work with the mind, but with specific focuses. To really meditate on the mind, however, we must go beyond it. The third gateway is the mind that transcends itself. To really gain nothing from Buddhist mind practice, we just need a little space.

> When you look upward into the space of the sky outside yourself,
> If there are no thoughts occurring or emanations being projected,
> And when you look inward at your own mind inside yourself,
> If there is no projectionist who projects thoughts by thinking them,
> Then your own subtle mind will become lucidly clear without anything being projected. Since the Clear Light of your own intrinsic awareness is empty, it is the Dharmakaya; and this is like the sun rising in a cloudless illuminated sky. Even though

this light cannot be said to possess a particular shape or form,
nevertheless, it can be fully known.
The meaning of this, whether or not it is understood, is
especially significant.

-Padmasambhava

To implement Guru Padmasambhava's instructions, I do what
we call in Dzogchen, Sky Gazing practice. You can actually do it
if you don't have any blue sky. But it's good to practice when you
find yourself under a blue sky, so you can visualize the sky during
meditation at other times, say when you're indoors. In the case
of being indoors, just meditate on the empty space before you.
For Sky Gazing practice, do a few rounds of deep, slow inhala-
tions and exhalations. Find a straight back but position yourself
so you can see as much unobstructed blue sky as possible without craning your neck.

Face the blue sky. Inhale, fill up. Open your mouth, exhale, release. Open
your eyes, and all of your senses. Be still and just suspend concepts for a few
moments. Look up at the sky. Ask yourself, "Is my mind like that?" Inhale
again. Open mouth exhale. Look at the blue sky. Relax deeply, everything
open to receive. Suspend your sense of self. Be empty. Gain nothing.

Repeat until enlightenment.

Journal Practice

- Based on what we've discussed so far, write about what refuge means to you.

- What have you taken refuge in?

- Where do you go for refuge on the levels of body, energy (emotions/speech), and mind?

- From the perspective of Buddhism, how can you integrate what you've been doing with a Buddhist sense of refuge?

- What is your level of interest in and commitment to your spiritual path at this point?

CHAPTER SEVEN

THE TWO ACCUMULATIONS

Life doesn't fit neatly into little boxes. Besides, they're all made out of ticky tacky. And they all look just the same. This year, I've lost everything, been homeless, couch surfed, been kicked out of two "safe" spaces by very crazy ladies after apparently not meeting their fantasy expectations, lost my sweetest dog, my long term partner, my mind, my dignity and quite a lot of my reputation. All of the pain is ego attachment. All of the meditation is about letting go. So here I sit, back in San Diego, trying again. I have my job, my yoga classes (so grateful for the practice and the students), my climbing gym. My heart is bigger than ever. My love for life is absolute. My meditation, and my back are strong. Yes, I'm in a complicated situation.

Love is simple in its principle yet complex in it's manifestation. I need to stay and give of myself completely. To me, that's what love is. I take refuge as best I can in my real nature, the state of freshness—open, raw, and timeless—without beginning or end. I take refuge in the Teacher, the Noble Arya Sangha, my shaman tribe, and in each step on this journey. We all suffer. We're all a fucking wreck. As my teacher said to someone, "This is samsara, what did you expect?" I open the four directions, call on all lineage holders, all Buddhas, Bodhisattvas, gurus, and healers of the three times. I call upon the Earth spirit, Pachamama, the spirit of the desert and the ocean, the mountains and the sky. I call upon all ancestors. Open this healing mandala. Come to us, help us. We need you. OM AH HUM. May we all be fully liberated immediately and without exception. Namaste.

-Darren Littlejohn, August 4th,
2015, Facebook Status

Merit and Wisdom

To gain merit in Buddhist practice means to accumulate positive karma. To gain wisdom is to realize emptiness, or to understand in a space beyond words that there is nothing, and there never was anything. It's all shimmering light, like the reflections of sunlight on the ocean. We can realize emptiness a little bit at a time, but let's not fool ourselves into thinking we're enlightened. If you think you are, you're not. But we can generate meditation experiences that support our progress. If they don't come, we don't worry. If they do, we nurture them like a little tiny baby in our arms. Then let them go and don't waste time trying to live in the memory of, "That one time before when the sky opened up and my mind was free and..." But we have to accumulate merit to attain wisdom.

We can't really accumulate merit if we don't give it away. In that regard, we're really not accumulating or gaining anything. We can gain wisdom, but unconventional wisdom. Buddhist wisdom is called the wisdom of emptiness. Emptiness is nothingness. To gain something is to gain nothing. To gain nothing is to gain the knowledge and wisdom that there is nothing to gain. In that sense, when we gain nothing, we gain an intangible something that is really a state of knowing about our real nature. It's not a gain you can put in your pocket. Do you understand the title of the book now? It's really all just words until we practice consistently to the point where we don't need to practice any more.

So merit in the Buddhist sense is positive karma in the karma bank. But it's still karma. We use karma to create merit and use merit to create more merit/karma. Merit gives us opportunity where we would otherwise have none. But *the ultimate state is beyond karma*. You don't hear that in conventional Buddhism. Dzogchen masters like Longchenpa teach this stuff. The natural state is beyond the body, breath and mind, but is the space-like nature—pervasive and without beginning. Think of gaining merit as a stepping stone. At the top of the ladder, you jump off into the unknowing. Sounds fun, right?

How do we gain merit? All of the things we've been talking about so far have been about gaining merit. All dharma study, meditation, practice, receiving teachings, doing positive actions with positive intentions and positive satisfactions—all of this creates merit. But it's kind of a slow process. There are ways to gain a lot of merit quickly. Offering is one. Purification is another. And always, dedication of merits at the end of practices (or beginning, or middle) will generate vast merits. I'll show you how to do all of these.

Just know that ultimately, it's about giving it away, not trying to hoard it for ourselves. That's the spiritual conundrum right there. It's about gaining nothing. Shh, don't tell your ego. She'll connive a way to convince you that it *really* is about gaining *something*. But that will be a lie.

Buddhism can seem intellectual, but is ultimately non-conceptual. What is non-conceptual? That's a state of consciousness that is beyond the mind. Past the mental landscape. Outside of ideas, but all-inclusive with infinite space. That kind of teaching may twist your mind or make you dizzy. But if you get it, even just for a moment, then you in a sense solve one level of the cosmic riddle (koan). In a Buddhist sense, you would then realize emptiness (remember this can happen in stages) and therefore gain nothing from Buddhist practice.

Everything we've discussed so far has led us to this point. But we could have started anywhere on any of these points as a portal into realization. Someone on Facebook asked me, "How many times do I have to do this practice (sky gazing) to become enlightened?" My answer: It depends. No one can answer that question for you. It depends on your merit, capacity, interest, commitment, the planets. If we understand the nature of samsara, we will have the desire to practice, *as if our hair is on fire*, as a Zen teacher said. If we still believe in our reality, namely that we can wrestle satisfaction out of this world if we only manage well, as we say in AA, well then we don't have much hope of getting out of the loop of suffering.

We need to understand the nature of suffering to be able to transcend suffering. That means that if we don't have the capacity to feel our own pain, then we'll never be able to heal it. And if we can't deal with our own healing, we aren't going to be much use to others on the path. The Buddha started his teaching with the Four Noble Truths. Life is suffering. We suffer for reasons. Reasons are causes. We can do different things to create different results. If we understand karma and do the correct things, we can completely eradicate our own suffering and the suffering of all beings. But if we still believe in our own BS, we will keep getting what we've been getting: more of the same.

My approach is deeply rooted in AA recovery (12-Step), Zen, Yoga and other energy practices, and Dzogchen. Dzogchen is called Ati Yoga. Ati means the highest. It's the highest yoga. Yoga is from one perspective a practice that means we unify our little self with our universal self. The negative with the positive. But in a Dzogchen sense, there's nothing to unify. We're already self-liberated. We just need to turn on the spiritual firehose, hang out with some really qualified, realized Masters, and obtain our own enlightenment. That is possible and doable because we live in a place and time where Buddhas manifest. Alternately, we can take our time and insist we need more convincing as we live our lives in pain.

Samsara will make a believer out of you later, if not sooner.

Most people who claim to understand something about Buddhism don't know it, but there are different views. They each come with their own perspectives, rules, paths, and practices. For example, some teachers would lead you through what is called a *graduated path*, "lam rim" in Tibetan. It's a step-by-step method that's been laid out over time by masters who included aspects of sutra teachings and tantra teachings. This is a Tibetan way of safely guiding practitioners through a series of realizations and practices to support those realizations. But it is a subtle infusion of sutra and tantra teachings. Most people don't know that or even what the difference is.

The sutra teachings are based on the first level of capacity of practitioners. These are ways of containing negative karma while creating new, positive karma. As I've discussed, these are methods of renunciation. That means to fully work the sutra program you not only have to meditate a lot, but you also need to restrict your actions of body, energy, and mind. This is an example of one view and it is the first level of Buddhist teachings. To gain anything, you sacrifice everything. This is ultimately true of all of the levels of Buddhist teaching, but the paths look different in the beginning stages. Those beginning stages can be several hundred million lifetimes, which, when you're talking infinity, makes sense. But in the sutra level, we don't talk about emptiness or going beyond mind or beyond time. Shhh. Those kinds of ideas will mess up the heads of your traditional Buddhist practitioners.

You do not need an initiation, transmission or even permission to study, or teach for that matter, on the sutra level path. Most Buddhism that's taught in the world is at this level. It's important that you understand the big picture. You can practice at any level that you want any time you want if you understand the comprehensive scope of the teachings. Otherwise, as my teachers have said, it's best to keep your mouth shut, try to be nice, and meditate a lot. That is also a path.

Tantra practices involve something more like magic. We work with energy (even sex), five elements, sacred syllables and words, images of enlightened beings, certain types of movements and gestures that communicate with enlightened beings and put us closer to their state. In this level of practice, we must have a qualified Vajra Master to guide us (I've listed some centers in the

Resources section of the book). If we don't, we run the risk of permanently fucking up our own energy. A lot of crazy people wander the streets. I personally don't want to wind up like one of them. So I don't go to any of these sex parties or polyamorous groups or tantric ritual gatherings that people like to have. I suppose I'm a bit conservative in that regard. But some tantric practitioners have used sex in very unconventional ways on their paths. If we're at a stage in our practice where we can really practice sex without attachment (but with skillful compassion) then sure. Maybe we're qualified. But most of us are addicted to sensations. To practice tantra with that level of attachment can really have negative consequences.

The practices of tantra ultimately involve working *with* energy rather than against it. Instead of blocking sensuality, we embrace it. If you watch a really sexy dancer either on a pole or the Discovery Channel doing some sort of South African ritual dance, you can get a sense of how we can use our body, movement, and sensual energy in a spiritual way.

Fundamentalists of some religions will tell you that this is all a sin and that you'll burn in hell or you should have your head chopped off or something if you practice like that. But they're insane. So you don't have to listen.

The higher level of Ati Yoga is a space where everything is self-liberated in its true nature. Nothing has a chance to hook in, accumulate, or cause problems when we live in this state of knowing. But as I've said, we can get little glimpses of this, and however life changing they may be, they're not the be-all end-all. If you really want to work with the Ati Yoga system, then you must find a qualified Dzogchen Master to give you what is called Direct Introduction. Some schools and systems negate that there is such a thing. But they're wrong. I've been working with it for over a decade and I can say with one hundred and ten percent certainty that this is a legit path. But if it scares you, do something less tricky. Follow your breath. Work with body meditations. They are good paths as well.

How to Gain Merit

Offering

An offering is something meaningful to us, not something we didn't want anyways. The more closely we cherish it, the more powerful the merit when we give it away. We can make offerings of the Three Gates; mentally, energetically, and physically. We offer to all of the Buddhas who have ever come and will ever come. Offerings can be formal, part of a long ritual, or informal. We might just pause for a moment and think, "I offer this up," whatever "this" is. We can use our imagination, our emotional experience, our money, our food. Offering is a very powerful tool. In the Tibetan practices such as Chod we offer our brains and guts (and everything else) and Tonglen where we willingly take on deadly illness and misfortune for the benefit of others. No one's asking you to do that, but those practices exist and you can find teachings and transmissions on them if you're interested.

One thing we can do very easily is make an altar. Find a little spot in your living space and create an altar with statues, images, candles, jewels, precious stones, and/or incense. Don't throw things on the altar. Treat it like the body of the Buddha. Nurture it like the soul of enlightenment. Your altar can be a power center for you. Just don't get attached to it. Build it and change it out often. You've seen the monks building Tibetan sand mandalas. They spend days meticulously building, only to sweep it all away when they're done. Everything is impermanent—teachings of the Buddha.

Put your altar in a high place on nice cloth. Even a small shelf will do. If you look on Instagram with some hashtags like #altar, you'll find a lot of examples. Make one. Make it your own. Add pictures of your teachers, sacred texts, precious items. I ask the ocean if I can take a little shell when I go to the beach. Those go on my altar. My old dog's tooth that fell out. Amazing Tibetan incense burns at every hour in my home. When I light the candle and incense, I look at the Buddha statue and say OM AH HUM many times. OM purifies the body. AH our energy. HUM the mind. OM AH HUM can be the only mantra that you ever use and the most powerful mantra that you'll ever need. You can use it to bless items that go on your altar. For the mantra to really work, try to get in front of a serious Tibetan master to get the oral transmission of the mantra. But saying it and using it may create the cause for you to find yourself in front of a teacher someday anyways. Meanwhile, practice and make offerings with an open heart and good intentions. You can find prayers or write your own. Here's one that I use:

To all the Buddhas and Bodhisattvas of the three times and the ten directions, I make offerings, prostrations, and go for refuge.

OM AH HUM

OM AH HUM

OM AH HUM

You can say it just like that. Light your candle mindfully. Put your palms together at heart center and say something like,

All beings suffer. May all beings be free of suffering. I will become enlightened and work for the benefit of all beings until there is no more suffering left.

Trust me, this creates oceans of merit. Oceans. You can keep flowers, fresh food, and money on your altar as offerings. Then take those off after a while and give them to other beings with the secret, silent blessing,

OM AH HUM may this being find a path out of suffering.

OM AH HUM may all beings be free of suffering.

OM AH HUM may I find a path out of suffering.

OM AH HUM may all beings be free of suffering.

Practice like that. It'll change everything. But don't trust me. Try it for yourself. If you're sincere, you'll see. Change the words if you like. Or ask a teacher to help you with a precrafted prayer, mantra, or system of offering.

You can offer anything; your food, your pain, your pleasure, attachment, struggle, fears, feelings, possessions. At any moment in your life, you can gain nothing by offering everything. Ultimately you'll give it all up. We give it away to accumulate merit. The more generous we are, the more we "gain."

Are you starting to get it? If not, just try to practice and see what happens.

Remember that karma transcends time. Lifetimes really. We reap the seeds we have sewn from beginningless time. Bad ones. Good ones. Sometimes simultaneously. So don't try to figure out what you did in this life to deserve what you're getting. It's probably a manifestation or ripening of karma from a long chain of lifetimes going back who knows how long. Just purify and practice in the now. That's all we've got anyways, right?

Jesus talked about it. What ye sow so shall ye reap.

But he didn't say when. There's often a long delay, so we have a hard time understanding why we experience certain things. So when you make offerings, don't give up if the immediate results that you expect don't arise. Instead of being demanding, be relaxed.

We've been accumulating karma through all of the six realms for endless aeons. We probably won't purify it all overnight. It's possible, but for most of us, we need to be patient and committed for a really long time. Try to be relaxed and self-liberate emotions as they arise. Make offerings. Be nice. Help people out. Bless bugs and animals—even and especially the food that you put in your mouth. Tell those beings under your breath,

OM AH HUM I know you suffered.

OM AH HUM I know you gave your life and I'm going to eat you.

OM AH HUM I have compassion for your suffering and will make this connection with you now. The next time we meet, I will be your guide.

May all beings be free of suffering.

OM AH HUM

OM AH HUM

OM AH HUM

That's pretty heavy practice right there—tantra in its essence.

Purification

We can clean out negative potentiality with purification practices. There are many practices. In my first book, I wrote about the Vajrasattva practice. There are many ways to purify. Some are more powerful than others. When we meditate, work on our compassion, contemplate emptiness, take refuge, or work with our pranayama, we also purify. When we make offerings, that too is a purification process. In fact, if we were to be in a state of contemplation even for a few moments, where we dwell in the experience of knowing that there is nothing to lose and nothing to gain—*rigpa in Tibetan*—we would purify aeons of negative karma. But if we can't do that in our stage of practice, we can do the things we've talked about already and that will help.

To do a more focused practice on purification, we can humble ourselves with prostrations before an image of the Buddha, sacred text, stupa, or altar. A stupa is a sacred structure and energy center that houses many powerful prayers and objects. Walking around a stupa clockwise (or counterclockwise in the

Bon tradition), called circumambulation, is a way of honoring its sacredness, which creates considerable merit. You can find stupas near Buddhist monasteries all over the world. You can also buy a tiny stupa figure for your altar.

Prostrations can be done partially, fully, or mentally. It can be done gross or subtle or even in secret. As you prostrate, you can imagine that you are infinite in number, making infinite prostrations and offerings to infinite Buddhas that permeate every atom of the universe. This is a very powerful use of our intention and creates massive amounts of merit.

Just put your palms together, get on your knees, crawl down to your belly, and stretch your two palms together in front of you, face down. Touch the back of your neck with your two joined palms, then come back to your knees and get back up with palms together at heart center. Touch your two palms to your crown to honor your guru (if you don't have one, you can just think Buddha), then touch the space between your eyebrows while saying OM to purify obscurations of the body. Touch your two palms to your throat while saying AH to purify obscurations of speech and then to your heart while saying HUM to purify obscurations of the mind. Pause there or continue doing prostrations until enlightenment.

In some systems, you'd be asked to do 100,000 prostrations to enter into that particular path of practice as preparation to receive higher teachings. This isn't really necessary, but it can be very useful. Some traditions are pretty strict about it. If you're going to participate in one of them, best to pay respect and do it their way. In fact, I'm planning to connect with some Nyingmapa who do *ngondro* (long term purification) practice and will probably do 100,000 of each of their purification practices. My teacher teaches that we should always work with circumstances. He says, "When it rains, we need an umbrella." When in Rome, we bust out our Dharma umbrella and do 100,000 prostrations. It's like that.

Dedication of Merits

As I've mentioned, I've been in Alcoholics Anonymous for over 30 years. One of our main principles is that we have to give it away to keep it. That means that in order to maintain our sobriety, which is contingent on the maintenance of our spiritual condition, we practice being generous, compassionate, and caring for others over ourselves. This is a pretty impossible practice for alcoholics like me, for whom selfishness and self-centeredness is the root of my problem. But that's also the best justification for doing such a practice.

You may ask why so many alcoholics and addicts rely heavily on going to meetings constantly if sobriety is contingent on our spiritual condition. If we're spiritual, why do we need meetings? In a way, I think it's because solo spiritual progress is too difficult for most people. It's really, really scary to live in the awareness of raw, naked presence with all of the character defects that get us into so much trouble in the first place staring us in the face. When we go to meetings, we can lean on the group for support. In a way, this keeps us stuck. It takes a true warrior spirit to leave the tribe and go into a lifetime of meditation practice where we meet life on life's terms without the safety net of the group.

I don't advocate that anyone should stop going to meetings. They're important. But over the past 8-10 years I find myself making more progress by doing daily yoga, body meditation, sky gazing and so on than sitting in meetings. But that's just my experience.

Whether we're in a sangha or walking the path as a solo yogi, all of us can benefit from the practices of letting go of self. In Zen, our practice is no-self. That means we gain nothing from Zen practice. In Tibetan Buddhist practice (and others), we always dedicate the merits gained from our meditation, study, and practice. That means we generate the feeling that whatever we've gained from the practice, we are totally willing to give that away for the healing of all sentient beings. It's kind of abstract, and I realize that not everyone has an ability to think abstractly. But if you can generate the willingness to give away whatever benefits that you get for yourself, you'll be on your way.

To dedicate the merits, we can say something at the end of a practice session, at the end of the day, or really at any moment. You can choose your own wording, but try to create the sentiment of giving it away, or gaining nothing.

Borrowing from tantra, we can use body, energy, and mind at the same time to triple up on the merits. When we put body, speech, and mind together in our practice, the power and effect of the practice can be stronger. In fact, it's even stronger on certain days. (You can get into Tibetan or Chinese or other forms of astrology to follow up on that.) Put your palms together, bow your head. That's the body practice. Use the words, such as I've suggested below. That's speech\energy. In your mind, cultivate the intention of letting go of clutching to your own sense of safety. If that's too hard, you can create an aspiration to be willing to give it away. If even that's a struggle, aspire to be willing to be willing!

May all beings benefit from this practice.

May my path of suffering and bliss be a path of liberation for all beings.

May all beings find a path out of suffering.

Here's mine:

I hope we can all help each other out and be kind. May anything that I've gained from walking this path be a force for healing on this planet and beyond.

Journal Practice

Write about what you really think you can gain in life.

- What can you gain physically?
- Can you gain anything energetically, emotionally?
- On a mental level, what can you gain?
- Of these things, what among them are truly sustaining?

To whom would you like to dedicate the merits from your practice?

Write your own personal dedication of merit, beginning with yourself, then with a loved one, and some friends, then the larger community of beings. See how far you can expand the feeling of wanting the best for others from the closest and most important to the wider, more general universe.

CHAPTER EIGHT

THE TWO TRUTHS

When one looks toward one's own mind -
The root of all phenomena -
There is nothing but vivid emptiness,
Nothing concrete there to be taken as real.
It is present and transparent, utter openness,
Without outside, without inside -
An all pervasiveness
Without boundary and without direction.
The wide-open expanse of the view,
The true condition of the mind,
Is like the sky, like space:
Without center, without edge, without goal.

By leaving whatever I experience,
Relaxed in ease, just as it is,
I have arrived at the vast plain
That is the absolute expanse.
Dissolving into the expanse of emptiness
That has no limits and no boundary,
Everything I see, everything I hear,
My own mind, and the sky all merge.
Not once has the notion arisen
Of these being separate and distinct.
In the absolute expanse of awareness
All things are blended into that single taste -
But, relatively, each and every phenomenon is distinctly,
clearly seen.
Wondrous!

-Shabkar

Relative and Absolute

Relative truth means that everything happens in relation to something else. Events don't occur all by themselves in a vacuum. Everything happens in context. Buddhists call this interdependence. Just think of relative as your normal, everyday dimension. We use our meditation to chip away at relative reality with our awareness until one day we see the light, literally, of absolute wisdom. But absolute knowledge isn't a place that you go to. There's no point A nor point B in the absolute. It is referenceless. A circle is often used to demonstrate the point.

We're always in the relative condition and the absolute at the same time. That's tricky to talk about and even trickier to really know in the sense of experiencing or knowing beyond mind and experience. Descartes said, "I think, therefore I am. But Buddhism says, "Even though I think, I'm really not." This, in Buddhism is considered the non-existent self. It thinks it's real. But it is not, as they say, inherently self-existent from it's own side. To know this is to gain nothing.

I work and practice and work and practice year after year and have had meditation moments of this knowing, but that's all. Moments are enough to keep you going though, as long as you don't get attached. It's like having an orgasm without being attached. When's the last time any of us did that? Just pause right in the middle of it and, without attachment, let go.

"Are you coming?"

"I was honey, but I just let it go instead so I can practice my non-attachment."

"I'm happy that you brought your spiritual practice into the bedroom. Now, make me come."

That's a good practice actually and pretty tough to do. If you follow any of the Taoist teachings of Mantak Chia and others, they teach many methods of working with our sexual energy in this way.

We can't really touch, taste, or feel absolute truth with the five aggregates, but it is right there. We can't *not* live in it. We are it. You hear things like this all the time, like that we're the expression of love in the universe. *One Love* bumper stickers sell by the millions. We love to talk up our spiritual game, even if we don't identify with having one. This is especially true in the yoga communities that I've been involved in. In a way, it's fake and superficial—even though it has many benefits. (I take class daily myself so I do endorse yoga, especially for meditators.) On some level, this talk is probably somewhat sincere. But even those who really commit to a path and try to practice constantly run into many obstacles. The old school dharma teachers never tried to sell it as some convenient solution for us to get more stuff to build up our egos. Instead, they refused students. Told them to go move a pile of rocks. Then go move them again. My teacher was already a well-studied famous scholar when he had a dream and somehow found his most important teacher. He sat there for days waiting for teachings. Then his teacher said, "Oh I already gave you those, in my dream on your first day." The teachings traditionally aren't handed to us for the asking. Students had to show their sincerity, seriousness, and commitment before they heard the first word. In the Tibetan systems, sometimes they ignore students until they make three requests for teachings. But there's so much out there these days and us Americans are so entitled, we want it all and we want it now and some people are ready to give it to all comers. But you get what you pray for. So be clear on what Dharma is and what you really want.

The path of Dharma in the West is often packaged and sold as a way to get more, not gain nothing. If the only spirituality you've dabbled in is a CorePower Yoga class or Law of Attraction webinar, this book might piss you off. Those things, have spiritual value to some people on some level, are not the real path, in and of themselves. *Oh no, this guy's talking from some spiritual hilltop.* Nope. Buddhism isn't about what people *should* do. The Buddhist path is logical. It's about what makes sense, not something that you should believe. It has a goal: transcend suffering. But the goal isn't something that you "get." There is nothing to gain. But it works if you work it. It's a real path, not a corporate program.

Remember, corporate programs want your money. The Dharma is about non-attachment. Those two goals are in direct opposition to each other. While you can benefit from such programs, I hope that you will try to understand the real meaning of the deep Dharma. Then you can take all the self-help, pseudo-spirituality weekend workshop stuff with a grain of salt, while still finding value in it.

The Dharma has nothing to do with acquiring material gain. Although tantra can be used for prosperity, that is not the end game. The Buddha didn't put anyone through a sales funnel. He didn't say, "OK, I'm going to tell you the secret, but first, have you heard of *The Secret?*" To my knowledge there was no Bonus or Bonus Bonus offer at the end of a sutra. And you didn't have to go through a $5k teacher training to learn what Dharma is really about.

The way I talk about Dharma teachings can be challenging. But don't shoot the messenger. I didn't invent these things. They are, however, based on a lifetime of study and practice of Buddhism in several different lineages. I'm not a real guru. I just tell it straight to the best of my understanding. In order to attract your interest, the real gurus will always hook you with the meat of the sweeter fruit. Once you get into the Dharma, you'll find that it has a bitter outer layer and nasty tasting pits. We somehow transcend the need to reject or accept either extreme. The spiritual path involves deep surrender. We never know how deeply we clutch until we find ourselves in the middle of the shit. The real path, the one that leads to absolute enlightenment (not a nine figure income), has sharp edges. There is no easier, softer way as we say in 12-Step. The only way around is through.

How to Find a Master

A master is a master of life. They're still in samsara, will still leave their physical body, and are subject to the conditions of the material world. But they're not subject to the same crazy crapola that dominates the rest of us. Masters exude the confidence of knowing *the real condition*. They exhibit kindness and compassion, but they can be fierce to get their point across. They're intelligent yet humble. They don't have a bunch of money, marital, or emotional issues governing their day-to-day lives. That's not to say they don't have money. Dharma Kings often have a lot of wealth. But they funnel it into their Dharma centers and not into mansions and sports cars.

So I'm kind of a Dharma middle man. May value to you is that I've had a lot of personal issues to overcome for my entire adult life. I'm a sober addict and come from an emotionally and physically abusive background. I make bad decisions based on that karma. I'm a practitioner, but I haven't mastered all of the aspects of my situation to the point where prosperity dominates my world. That said, I've been clean and sober almost 19 years. You're reading my fourth book. I've been a yoga teacher for over five years and I feel comfortable in my own skin. But a master I am not.

Masters are the kinds of people who when they walk into a room, people gravitate to them. They want to ask the master things and be in their presence. As I said, they embody the teaching. Me, I'm just a traveler on the path. I have a way of being able to explain things, but I don't really want to be anyone's "teacher." I coach people, lead retreats, teach meditation. But some people who came up around the time I did have developed centers, training systems, programs and have otherwise set themselves up pretty well. That's not my path. That said, I'm be happy to coach

anyone who asks for help. You can find me online at http://
darrenlittlejohn.com if you're interested in help getting started
or maintaining your spiritual program. But you need a real guru
to make real progress.

I've talked a lot about the kind of teachers that you want to
watch out for. But the legitimate teachers are out there. You have
to be discerning to find them. Be prepared to make mistakes. I
know of plenty of practitioners who've followed knuckleheads
for years before they found a real Dharma teacher. That is part
of the process. We all go through it to some degree or another.
You should be aware of the different levels of teachings such as
I've described, and the meaning of lineage as well as the politics
involved in hierarchies. Read up on the histories of Tibetan and
other branches of Buddhism.

A word of caution: avoid any groups, teachers, or books affili-
ated with anyone who speaks out against His Holiness the Dalai
Lama. Bad news. Consider yourself warned. Some of those people are bad news. Very bad news.

So how do we get to the absolute from the relative if there's
nowhere to go and nothing to gain? Meditation. Study. Practice.
And we have to understand suffering by experiencing our own
suffering and feeling the suffering of all conscious beings.

News Meditation

Contemplate the tragic story below that came out in the news
recently. You can use items like this, or any of the plethora of
terrible sufferings that go on in our world, to practice. See if
you can use it to contemplate suffering and apply some of the

principles we've been working with. For example, read the passage several times. Notice the body sensations, your breath, the thoughts as they float by like clouds in the sky. Allow yourself to get deeper into the core feelings around this level of suffering. Find compassion. Notice anger, but don't cultivate anger towards the aggressors. Pray for their release from samsara. Do Buddhists pray? Sure. Some do. Some don't. I have on many occasions. You can choose.

What comes out of this massive and detailed dossier is a tale of horror in which Mao emerges as one of the greatest mass murderers in history, responsible for the deaths of at least 45 million people between 1958 and 1962. It is not merely the extent of the catastrophe that dwarfs earlier estimates, but also the manner in which many people died: between two and three million victims were tortured to death or summarily killed, often for the slightest infraction. When a boy stole a handful of grain in a Hunan village, local boss Xiong Dechang forced his father to bury him alive. The father died of grief a few days later. The case of Wang Ziyou was reported to the central leadership: one of his ears was chopped off, his legs were tied with iron wire, a ten kilogram stone was dropped on his back and then he was branded with a sizzling tool — punishment for digging up a potato. -Washington Post, August 3rd, 2016

Can you try to sit and imagine a handful of these experiences for a few moments, just to gauge the magnitude of suffering for all beings? Does this give rise to compassion, or just anger, frustration, and despair? Where is the emotion arising from? Where does it go? Notice empty space. Allow yourself to relax in the space of primordial emptiness without agitation.

This is very excellent practice.

If the news upsets you, make it a regular practice to practice with it. *OK, I'm turning on the news now for my meditation. No getting carried away. Breath, notice, relax.* Remember, it's all relative. The news will upset you, especially the more sensitive you get with consistent meditation. But the more sensitive that you get, the deeper your awareness has to go.

Some teachers talk about teachings as fingers pointing at the moon. This is one way of saying that words are inadequate to describe—even symbolically—the actual experience of the state of realization, or any of the preliminary states that lead up to it. Even the experience of realization is still in the realm of samsara. To attain Buddhahood is to transcend samsara, which is to transcend mind and mental states and the need for a point of view or an experience. This kind of teaching may stretch your brain, like our koan practices. You may think, "Why did the lady drive drunk into the front of the bar?" I mean that really happened in my neighborhood not long ago. But we'll never answer that question. See, the news is about behavior and the "why "is a koan. But viewing the news this way is intended to actually take you beyond the mental state, even if just for a split second. You can nurture that tiny fraction of time into the full blown dilio. Remember, the tools are intended to transcend themselves, but that isn't likely to happen right away. Trust me, there's plenty more news to come. You'll never be short on meditation material.

Since everything is relative but exists in the absolute, all phenomena are said in the teachings to be inseparable. Practice gets us deeper into this knowledge. When we can get into and remain in that state of deeper knowledge, our situation in life can change drastically for the better.

If you find yourself having a lot of trouble as you practice more and more, seek out an initiation of Vajrasattva (see *The 12-Step Buddhist*, 2009) or another purification deity and commit yourself to a series of practices and purifications, called *ngondro* in Tibetan. Some of the teachers mentioned above do these ngondro retreats regularly. If you have the time, finances and opportunity, go for it.

We must find a good situation and work on purifying our obstacles in order to gain anything and ultimately gain nothing from Buddhist practice. It's fine to go your own way, get some books, meditate a little. But it'll take longer. And none of us knows when the moment of our death will arrive. If you can get into a serious teaching and commit yourself to a long term practice, the results will happen. It's impossible not to succeed. But it's much easier if you follow an accomplished master than if you try to do it on your own with books and buddies. Although study and spiritual friends are important on the path of practice, having a great teacher will literally cut through the haze of samara and our karmic delusions. However, it can be a painful process.

We don't even know how deeply we grasp in our relative, dualistic condition, until what we're grasping onto is ripped away. Strong teachers and strong practice will show you these attachments. They have for me. This isn't done normally in a one-on-one session where they do some kind of cover-pulling reality therapy. But it is reality therapy and it does pull our covers. The Vajra Master works within you, along with protectors and deities. The process is internal and deeply psychological. Without a strong foundation in practice, a good support system and a healthy lifestyle, you can go crazy on this kind of path. That said, even some Zen students and masters go crazy and their path isn't initiation-related or energy based. The point here is that when you do the work, the shit will hit the fan. Be ready for it. It's a path to end suffering, but you go through suffering, not around it. It's the spiritual equivalent of no pain, no gain.

It's kind of like doing a workout. We strain and tear our muscles apart and are sore the next day. During the recovery period, the muscles repair and wind up stronger. If we stay at our comfortable weight, we might do a little maintenance, but not make a lot of progress. Having a master teacher is like having a pro-Olympian as your personal trainer. But instead of just meeting at the gym for an hour a week, he's in your head and your heart and your soul—even in dreams.

How it works is this: pain happens. We relax and don't avoid it. We take refuge in our guru, the Buddha, Dharma and Sangha. Then, repeat until enlightenment.

CHAPTER NINE

INTEGRATION: THREE PRACTICES

We live in illusion and the appearance of things. There is a reality. We are that reality. When you understand this, you see that you are nothing, and being nothing, you are everything. That is all.

- Kalu Rinpoche

Awareness, Intention and Focus

We've discussed some major topics in Buddhism to this point: The Three Poisons, Five Aggregates, Three Gates, Two Truths and so on. The three of these and two of those nomenclature was designed to help practitioners remember teachings, especially in those times when nothing was written down, let alone recorded for YouTube. I've given exercises for you to explore their meanings on deep levels. In this chapter, I'd like to offer a program that can be followed by an individual or group of interested meditators. With these basic principles and practices of Buddhism integrated into one brief system of study and practice, you can feel confident that you are on a path. If you're already well on your way, then I hope this gives you a fresh perspective and a deeper understanding.

Remember that the main point of Dharma practice is total liberation from suffering for all beings, forever.

In the past few years, I've moved from teaching meditation in groups and retreats to incorporating it into my yoga classes. It started in a Sunday morning class at 24 Hour Fitness here in downtown San Diego. Since it was morning, I wanted to meditate so I opened the class that way. It made me feel good and the students got right into it. It eventually became the opening to every class I'd teach. My boss started coming to class to check up on me as the managers do with all of the fitness instructors. But she wound up being a regular.

These meditations can't help but come from a Buddhist orientation. But we don't talk Buddha in the gym. I had to be very careful what language I used, so I learned to simplify the principles in order to benefit rather than alienate anyone. These meditations became the basis for a talk, which as I mentioned became the basis for this book. Now that we've discussed much of what goes into the dynamics of our meditation practice (something that would be impossible in a 10 minute meditation at a gym), we can integrate all aspects of the practice in the same simple manner. But, know that these practices are missing nothing. They are as profound, deep, and potentially illuminating as any meditation that I've done with masters. They are also connected to those lineages.

These practices of body, speech (energy), and mind can be done individually. But remember that our body, speech, and mind are inseparable. The way I teach meditation may start sometimes from one point of view and at others, from a totally different perspective. You can mix and match, alternate between views and tools and do them in any order for any length of time. It's your path. I'm just walking on it right next to you. It's up to you, as we say in AA, to take the steps.

What I'd like to offer here is a program that you can follow by yourself or with a group. I've found over the years that most people need some direction. I can give you a grab bag of things to try, but maybe you'd like a daily formula to follow. Try it, but don't feel obligated to keep it intact exactly as I've laid it out here. As I said, I'd be happy to help guide you if you need help.

At least in the beginning, the three levels of practice are awareness, intention, and focus. We can do them all at once or in any combination. The more stable our meditation, the better off we are in staying grounded as we direct ourselves towards one application or the other. I'm going to give you a sample daily practice below. It will be very Buddhist in orientation. But as I've said all along, you need to be aware of the limitations of different sects and the challenges that some practitioners have made to traditional, classic systems. This is particularly true of those wild yogis in the Vajrayana (and even before it was called that). Some didn't even identify as Buddhist or Hindu or being part of a lineage. It's important to read translations of ancient texts to understand the history and hagiography of these streams of teaching. This is crucial when you find yourself with a group or a teacher who seem to be convinced that their way is the only right way or that they follow the One True God. The truth is, as Zen author Brad Warner just pointed out on Facebook recently, that we're all Buddhas. We follow a teaching that will lead us out of hell, until we realize the fruit of that teaching. Namely, that we're already self-perfected in our natural state. Buddha. No questions to ask.

I'm not a group guy, unless I'm leading it. Some people (teachers) often don't like me in their groups because I question everything. Buddha questioned the established hierarchies of his day, so why shouldn't I? I don't want to cause too much trouble, though, so

I tend to stay away from groups or form my own. I belong to two international sanghas and have spent years doing service. But these days, I tend to practice alone. That will likely change again. But my point to you is that you don't have to be attached to how your practice looks, as long as you continue to practice. Everyone has a different way of learning and dealing with their own karma.

You probably won't do well if you bounce all over and never commit to anything. You might try a particular meditation, teacher, or group and stick with them for ten or twenty years. Just do it knowing that you are free to change your course when the conditions are right for that. My friend spent a good ten years looking for a guru and never committed. I think he will likely be reborn in a place and time where there will be teachings, because he spent a lot of time doing purification and collecting merits. I'll say to you what I said to him. Relax. The right answers will come. I was told not to push. Breathe in. Breathe out. Try not to be a dick.

Daily Practice

I'll give some detail on how to do the practices below but you're already familiar with most of the principles from earlier chapters. If you prefer one of these previous exercises, feel free to substitute. At the end, I'll give some sample sessions that you can use for individual or group practice. Check the book's website for more meditations that aren't in the book, as well as the meeting guide that I mentioned in the beginning. I have an email list that you can sign up for on the site where you can stay in the loop on things.

Journal Practice

Begin with a short, three to five minute journaling session. Do a check-in with yourself. Write down some questions about your life that you'd like answers to. Here are some examples. Feel free to use any of these or ask your own. You can also just write freely for five minutes on whatever thoughts and feelings come up. Just write.

- What am I missing?
- What needs clarity?
- Who do I want to be?
- Who needs forgiving?
- What are my strengths today?
- Where do I want to improve?
- Why am I meditating?
- Where is the path?

Awareness Practice

Note that in the awareness practices, we're not using intention or focus. Just notice. Later, when you can taste the difference through experience and practice, you'll be able to integrate the different practices. They do build on each other. So when we do a pranayama practice, we definitely have awareness. When we're focused, we're using intention. The reason we do them separately at first is to build a foundation.

Awareness with Body, Speech (Energy), and Mind Body Awareness

Sit in a comfortable position with a straight back. Commit to being physically still for a set period. Set a timer for at least 20 minutes. Let your hands rest in your lap, palms up to be open or palms down if you need to feel more grounded. Let your eyes settle on the space in front of you and close them halfway. Notice your toes, feet, and ankles. Bring your awareness up your legs, into your pelvic region, waist, belly, and chest. Notice your fingertips, forearms, elbows, and shoulders. Feel the space between your shoulder blades. Let your awareness run up and down your spine, to the top of your head, ears, jaw, lips, to the tip of your nose. Feel inside your mouth while remaining still. Inside your nose, ears. On your scalp. Continue scanning the body. Notice sensation without decisions. Feel the density of your muscles, joints, and bones.

Take your awareness deeper. Let it move into the spaces of your organs, cells, and blood flow. Without effort or thought, let your awareness permeate the spaces between your nerve fibers, synapses in the brain, and connective tissues. Be in the space between molecules that make up the physical body. Relax deeply into the physical dimension.

Pose the questions:

- What does my body have to gain?

- What can it lose before it ceases to be my body?

- If I don't move at all, how do I know my body exists?

Graduate level PhD work would be if you can notice that the body is empty. It's nothing. It doesn't exist in and of itself and is definitely not what we think it is. To gain nothing, we gain an awareness of the nothingness of the body. We gain knowledge of nothing, in the sense that there is nothing but space. Even space is just a concept. Eventually, even that sense of knowing, no matter how deep, will dissolve into emptiness so that there is nothing left but pure, timeless awareness.

Buddhists call this the realization of emptiness or the attainment of the Wisdom of Emptiness.

Energy (Breath) Awareness

Do this practice in 20 minute sessions.

Assume your meditation position. This practice can be done while moving as well. But it's best to get a good foothold on it by learning it while sitting still.

Notice the belly as it rises and falls. Notice the air as it comes in through your nostrils. Be aware of the breath in the back of your throat. Notice the air in your lungs.

- Where is it?

- Where does it come from?

- Where does it end?

- Who is breathing?

Next Level: Notice your energy as it moves through your body. Look for the connection between your breath and your energy.

Notice your emotional state. Without necessarily adding words, explore the sensation of emotions as they circulate through your body.

What part of the body do you feel emotions in?

Label it. If you can, put your hand there. If not, get a massage and recall this mediation during the massage. You can also record yourself reading a meditation and listen to it on headphones during a massage.

Return to the practice of breath\energy\emotional awareness throughout the day, as often as you can remember. Go to sleep with it. Keep that awareness in your dreams. Wake up with it. Repeat.

Mind Awareness

Do this one in 20 minute sessions. You can also do this for 20 seconds at a time throughout the day.

Sit still. Notice the body. Notice the breath. Notice the thoughts. They are like reflections of sunlight on the ocean. Relax as they shimmer. Stay aware without being hypnotized by your thoughts. Don't follow or develop thoughts. Just let them come and go. Remember, this is not the same as rejecting thoughts or trying not to think.

- Where do your thoughts come from?

• Where do they go?

Intention with Body, Speech (Energy), and Mind

The difference between awareness practice and practice with intention is that in our awareness, we just practice with what is, as it is. We don't change or try to fix anything. It really is a difficult thing to do, or not do as the case may be. Our minds are always trying to gain something. If we tell the mind, "Hey, there's nothing to gain," the mind will rebel and try to move on to more fertile ground.

When we set our intention, however, we do intend—by definition—to obtain a result. Normally we don't set intentions, they set us. Unconscious drives rule us from deep within, based on aeons of karma. The Buddhist practice of setting intention is based on mindfulness, rather than an impulse. Though we may have the impulse to benefit other beings, when we work with our intention as part of our Dharma practice, along with awareness, the practice—and the karmic result of that practice—is more powerful. Remember, to generate strong karma, we need intention (fueled by awareness, meditation, study, and realization at whatever level), the action itself, and satisfaction about the result.

When we practice a lot of Dharma with mindful awareness, self-examination (or no-self), and an educated mind on the teachings of the Buddha, we can generate a lot of merit. Remember, the only point of generating merit is to gain nothing. We call gaining nothing the Wisdom of Emptiness. Awareness sets up the ground for establishing strong intention. Intention established the basis for an action, or karmic deed. We know what we're doing, we do it, and we can feel good about what we did. And then we can give it away in our dedication. You're seeing the point by now I hope. If not, keep practicing.

While we can begin after awareness practice, the practice of intention can also be done as a stand-alone practice. We can be open and creative in finding ways to cultivate good intentions with body, speech, and mind.

Body Intention

Your body moves all day. How often does it move with purpose and intention? Lama Zopa says that if we can make each movement of the body an aspiration for the enlightenment of all beings, we create merit constantly. We can think of innovative ways to dedicate the movements of our body with the intention to benefit all beings.

- As I take each step, may all beings also step onto the path of Dharma.

- Standing up, may compassion rise up in the hearts of all beings.

- As I sit, may all beings take the seat of a Buddha.

- Going to sleep, may all beings who suffer wake up from the dream of samsara.

- As I touch this person, may they be touched by compassion and receive infinite blessings from infinite Buddhas.

Those are a few ideas. Write four of your own!

1. _____

2. _____

3. _____

4. _____

Sit with Intention

As we've done already in our seated meditation practice, we can find a comfortable seat kneeling, half or full cross-legged, or on a chair. Our intention is to sit mindfully with a straight back. Draw the belly in. Tuck the tailbone down. Lift the chest. Shoulders up and back and down. Back of the neck is long. Chin tucked. Eyes half shut (or half open if you're an optimist).

Sit like this any time. Doesn't have to be a formal meditation session. It's good for your spine. If you meditate a lot in this position, whenever you go into it, you'll be able to lock in your Zen. Try it. Let me know how it goes.

Stand with Intention

Mountain Pose is one that we do many times in every yoga class. Stand with feet separated, hips-width distance. Feet parallel. Lift the toes and drop them back down, one at a time. Press your arches down, firmly, with the intention to be grounded. Lift your kneecaps slightly. Rotate the thigh bones inward, towards the center line. From the hips upward, adopt the same principles as your meditation seat. Rotate your palms outward. Option: place your palms together at heart center. Assume this pose for a few breaths or longer.

You can go into this pose any time, just from the waist down or just doing the shoulders. If you're standing in line, it will help you take pressure off of your lower back. These postures have many health benefits. The point is to stand with mindful intention, wherever and whenever you find yourself. If you don't remember how at any given point, just say, "Standing with intention, my feet are on the earth."

Walk with Intention

Zen Master Thich Nhat Hanh says to let your feet massage the earth with compassion as you walk. You might check your intentions as you walk.

- Am I stomping on the earth like I own it and am crushing it beneath my feet?

- Do I walk on eggshells most of the time?

- How can I walk with the intention to be of benefit?

- Can I feel the details of my soul in each step. (See what I did there?)

Set your intention as you walk. With each step, say to yourself, "May all beings walk the path of liberation."

Eat with Intention

Food is a charged topic in Buddhism. I've written about this in detail before (The Power of Vow, 2013), and there are good books on mindful eating such as Jan Chozen Bays, Mindful Eating: A

Guide to Rediscovering a Healthy and Joyful Relationship with Food. I won't get too heavy here about the ethics of eating. When you eat, ask yourself:

- Am I a greedy gobbler or a mindful masticator?

- How can I appreciate the lives that were given in the production of this food?

- Can I practice gratitude for each bite?

Set an intention:

I need to eat to be healthy. I need to be healthy to serve beings. By taking care of myself, I'm making myself fit to be of service.

Breathe with Intention

We can shift our intention when breathing so that we breath in a directed manner. We've done some pranayama already. There are many specific and detailed practices of pranayama from different traditions. From yoga, the famous teacher B.K.S. Iyengar says, "The yogi observes details like time, posture and even breath rhythm and is alert and sensitive to the flow of prana within him." Beyond being observant and alert, we can breathe more fully and complete.

Going back to our earlier practice, we can add the intention of the breath with a simple aspiration.

- Breathing in, I wish for all beings to be safe and cared for.

- Breathing out, may all suffering be expelled from every living creature on the Earth.

- Breathing for all beings

- Breath for all beings

- Love for all beings

Our pranayama *ujaii* also works for breathing with intention. That's the slight constriction at the back of the throat on both the inhalation and the exhalation.

We can breathe slower and deeper. Hold the breath on the inhale and the exhale.

Breath in for a count of four. Hold full for a four count. Exhale for four and hold empty for four. Repeat. This practice always works to calm me down. You can increase the number of counts slowly over time, but be careful. Pranayama overdone can cause negative problems. All the master teachers warn of this.

Think with Intention

Change your thoughts, change your karma. Bad thoughts bring negative karma, good thoughts bring merit. I haven't discussed it here because it's been written about ad nauseum, but the Buddha taught in the Noble Eightfold Path as the last of the Four Noble Truths about right view, right intention, right speech, right action, right livelihood, right effort, right mindfulness, and right concentration. The Buddha to my knowledge didn't teach about the power of positive thinking, at least not as it's been called by the law of attraction people. But think about it. How much mental karma do we create with our thought energy?

While the teachings say that we need intention, action, and satisfaction, thought has power to create karma—even indirectly. My old AA sponsor taught me back in the 80's that before we do anything, we at some level give ourselves permission. That means if I harbor negative thoughts about someone, it creates a tone in my mindset towards that person, people like that person, triggers that remind me of that person, ad infinitum. One little cause can snowball into bigger causes that can result in feelings which eventually inform actions. The positive thinking movement would have us believe that any thought creates our reality. Buddhism sees it differently. Thoughts have effects and those effects serve to further our delusion that we're really who we think we are.

In the Dharma, thoughts don't create reality, they can only attempt to describe it, analyze it, change it, or control it. Thoughts are the last thing we should consider real. Yet the practices on the mind are the most difficult. The mind is, after all, invisible and made up of many layers, most of which are beneath our awareness. Meditation brings these things to the surface. So the idea of creating intention in the mind has very powerful ramifications. Even if we don't believe in some thoughts that we use to create intention, we can train our brains and our minds to think along the lines of positivity and compassion.

For example, if I have a resentment against someone, I can practice Dharma to change the intention of my thinking.

Resentment: *Joe is a jerk. He did x, y and z to me.*

New Intention: *I want to see Joe as a person just like myself, who doesn't want so suffer. Somehow I'd like to understand him better and resent him less.*

Notice that it's OK to start small. You don't have to jump from, "Joe is a jerk," to "Oh my God, I'm so in love with Joe." You can use the aspiration to compassion. That's more real than fake, superimposed compassion and will create a karmic thought-feeling reaction in your mindstream.

Hey I'd like to be open minded about Joe. He must have valid reasons that make sense to him.

You can act "as if," as many people say, but in the Dharma we try to see it not *as if* but *as is*. Then we meet ourselves where we are to create a new intention.

Yeah, so by being attached to my feelings about Joe, I'm probably creating more suffering for myself and others. What do I need to do to create an opposite mental action? Much better than lying to ourselves by saying Joe is such a wonderful soul who wants to blossom just like a lotus. Joe's probably a jerk. But we are also jerks. As soon as we create a new aspiration to deepen our understanding, our wisdom and our compassion, we set the karmic ball in motion to a happier way of life.

By studying the principles laid out in this and other Dharma or spiritual books, you're already exercising some kind of intention. The big intention in Dharma is to live in the truth, rather than the hypnotic spell of our mental fantasies.

Below is the best example that I know of for how to practice mental intention. The possibilities for how you can apply this are limitless because suffering beings are limitless as are their sufferings. If you learn how to internalize this ideal, you'll be able to apply it in many different ways. Don't be surprised if many new opportunities to practice compassion jump up in your path when you start this practice of thinking with the bodhisattva's intention.

His Holiness Dalai Lama calls this Generating the Mind for Enlightenment. I took this vow with him live in 2006 in San Francisco. Recite it three times per session. Do this session three times a day.

With a wish to free all beings,

I shall always go for refuge

to the Buddha, Dharma and Sangha

until I reach full enlightenment.

Enthused by wisdom and compassion,

today in the Buddha's presence

I generate the Mind for Full Awakening

for the benefit of all sentient beings.

As long as space endures,

as long as sentient beings remain,

until then, may I too remain

and dispel the miseries of the world.

If all of that is too much for you, I get it. It is powerful, and it will change your karma and your life. But if it's too hard, don't worry. One thing you can do is make a list for yourself of some ways that you can upgrade your vibration by setting the *aspiration* for a higher intention. Here are some ideas:

- May I think kind thoughts.
- May I be gentler to myself in my heart and mind.
- May I think with compassion about myself and others.

- May I practice mental generosity.

- May I aspire to be less angry.

- May I aspire to acquire more patience.

- May I think in possibilities, rather than limitations.

- I aspire to be loving.

- I aspire to be slow to react.

- I aspire to give strength to those who need it.

- I aspire to connect my heart to the hearts of others.

Focus with Body, Speech (Energy), and Mind

While we can practice awareness or intention any time, they really do depend on each other. So it's helpful to separate them out in practice. Just know that it's kind of arbitrary and you can work with it however is best for you. We've practiced the awareness and intention together quite well so far. Let's wrap up this chapter, and the book, by integrating focus for body, speech (energy), and mind.

Body Focus

When we practice awareness, the objective is to simply be aware of whatever is happening. We can focus our awareness on one object, or let it be global and all encompassing. As we consciously shift our intention, our movement, our presence and our physical experience we have the opportunity to gain wisdom (nothing). What does it mean?

We can have focus *on* the body. The shift here isn't that the body is in a particular stance, such as Second Warrior in a yoga series. But it's more like our mind is focused with our awareness and intention, on a particular aspect of the body. This isn't a hatha yoga book, so I won't go into detail on postures, but if we go back to our simple Standing at Attention Pose, we can work with the energy of focus as an example. You can actually do this in any pose, no matter what position you find yourself in. Doesn't have to be a yoga pose. But this is a great place to start. If you happen to practice hatha yoga already, this will enrich your practice.

Assume the posture, same as in the Stand with Intention exercise. Stand with feet separated, hip-width distance. Feet parallel. Lift the toes and drop them back down, one at a time. Press your arches down, firmly, with the intention to be grounded. Lift your kneecaps slightly. Rotate the thigh bones, inward, towards the center line. From the hips upward, adopt the same principles as your meditation seat. Rotate your palms outward. Option: place your palms together at heart center.

Move through the three practices by focusing on their different aspects. Once you get into the posture, before moving deeper, just be aware of the soles of the feet on up the legs through the hips, belly, back, shoulders, arms, fingertips back up to the neck, face, and head. Notice the sensation on the surface of your skin. What is the temperature like? Feel where clothing touches your skin. Take your awareness deeper, into the muscle tissues, joints, bones, organs, and cells. Be *in* that awareness of the body.

Create intention. *My intention is to be gentle, strong, compassionate, and patient.* Now focus. The practice here is called *pratyahara*.

According to yoga scholar David Frawley, pratyahara is not only the withdrawing of the senses, but:

Pratyahara is twofold. It involves withdrawal from wrong food, wrong impressions, and wrong associations, while simultaneously opening up to right food, right impressions, and right associations.

From a Buddhist yogi perspective, we choose to focus our attention *and* our intention on the posture and our deep physical being *to the exclusion* of all else. That's what we mean by focus. First, be still. Be aware. Take the awareness deeper, so deep that you don't notice any outside stimuli.

Try just doing this with your fingertip at first. Hold it up and look at it or just close your eyes and feel it. Push out any other thoughts, feelings, or sensations for five seconds. Be present in that awareness alone. Then relax. Repeat. Focus your awareness with the intention to hone your concentration. You can fuel that intention with an aspiration statement, something like this:

May I develop the concentration of a Buddha so that I may use it to study and practice Dharma for the benefit of all beings.

OM AH HUM

As always, feel free to write your own aspiration, ask your teacher, or find one in a book. You'll also see in Buddhist literature, especially Japanese Zen, a vast emphasis on concentration abilities. We need an unwavering mind so that we're undistracted. Then samsara can't suck us into its infinite quicksand, distracting us away from our real nature. Make sense?

You can practice this laser concentration in sessions of just a few minutes, with very short but strong periods of concentration and relaxation. My teacher says that if we do this for a few days on a retreat, we can get some pretty good results very quickly. Your results may vary, but give it a shot.

Feel free to also choose a different body part. I know what you're thinking, and I didn't say that! But seriously, practice body focus in your Mountain Pose, with your finger, your toe, the end of your nose. Take up yoga and work that focus on your whole body in all of your classes. It'll help!

Breath\Energy Focus

Since we've worked a lot with the breath already and haven't touched on many of the afflictive emotions, let's go ahead and link our breath practice to our emotional state using the integration of Awareness, Intention, and Focus (AIF).

First we become aware of the breath, then we direct the breath with intention. This becomes a sharp focus as we control the flow of prana through our body and our energy system. Focus becomes a stepping stone to higher meditative states. Recall that in the sutra system, there is little if any breath training, except to be aware of the breath. Of course over the millennia, many derivations and combinations of practices have formed. But in the more direct lineages, there remain many divisions. Manipulation of the breath is one of them.

For example, in the Vajrayana, when using mantra and focus, the state of samadhi—that non-dual oneness—is reached. Then more and more subtle levels of dualistic thinking are abolished until full realization. As my own practice has evolved in recent years, I've been able to direct prana by using these techniques to elevate my state of body, emotions, and mind. I begin with breath and body awareness, then move to a head check. *How is my thinking right now?* The awareness set-up creates a base for some intention work. *OK, notice a non-dual state.* Then set intention. *Let's be present in that state without altering or modifying it.* Then back to simple awareness. When I (which is non-separate and non-existent) notice that there's a particular way of focusing my attention in that state, it's then possible to refine that focus. *Look deeper. Enter into that space. Be in that space.* Then rest in pure, naked awareness.

It takes some time and skill to be able to shift back and forth like this. You might have the capacity to do it it right away. But if you don't, it's OK. Just work on one of the practices at a time. I've been doing this work for over thirty years so don't expect that your experience will be the same. In fact, your experience is totally different, and totally valid. Just chill in that space, however it is.

So you can see that the process of awareness, intention, and focus has some basis in sutra and tantra. If you study any hatha yoga, you'll know that pranayama is a big part of the training, particularly in the less corporate studios. But you do have to find a valid teacher who practices a well-established system for it to work well and safely.

*Note that newer practices like the hyperventilation techniques of (holotropic) some LSD-addled psychologists do not count as pure lineage—Buddhist or otherwise. I'd steer clear of those things. I have heard of some practitioners who got good results with these techniques but I have no experience with them. I just find the idea of hyperventilating for two hours to get into some state where you see past lives is a little scary. But as you wish.

For our purposes, we want to create very sharp focus with the breath as it relates to our emotional state. Keep in mind that we're not trying to eradicate the feelings. We're using our breath to transform the emotional states. That's different. We don't try to block out the feelings. But we bring them up in the fire of the breath and let the energy change into something clean and useful rather than toxic and destructive.

Use this practice when you're not agitated to prepare you for times when you really need it. Then when it hits the fan, you'll have a basis of familiarity to work from. I've used this myself to transform some pretty serious emotional pain.

To begin, notice the body, breath and mind. If you need clarity, do a little journaling or have some kind of therapeutic session to help. That could be talking to a friend, counselor, coach or sponsor, listening or playing music, or whatever brings you some connection to your feelings.

Notice the feelings in the body. How do they connect to your emotional state? Without really trying to label or name your emotion, just notice it. The connection to emotion is always in the body and the breath. Notice it without words. Settle in on this emotional feeling. Notice it. Breathe normally, then deep and full. Watch the breath. Bring up the feeling. Follow it. Follow the breath. Now, with your intention, think that you want to send the prana into the center of the feeling space by using your directed breathing. This is somewhat symbolic and total energy work.

So it's less tangible perhaps than some of the earlier practices. Tantra or yoga teachers often say to *breathe into* the space of the root chakra or lower back. It's like that. We're noticing our feelings and breathing life energy into them.

Create that focused constriction at the back of the throat. Think of the energy of your prana moving into the feeling space. It's like the finger exercise where we focus on a single object. We're doing the same here, but internally, with a thing that isn't a tangible thing but an energy.

Do this kind of practice in short sessions, for just a few moments at a time. Then go back to awareness. Then when you notice feelings again, relax, go deeper, move the prana into the space of the emotion. To generate merit and therefore gain nothing, you can think something like *may this practice benefit all beings*, or, *I'm purifying this emotion so that I may be more compassionate.*

You can add this practice to your sessions or try it any time during the day. First thing in the morning works well too. Another way you can do this kind of work is to get very still first, then work on a short focus session for short periods of time. Set the meditation timer (there are apps for that) for 20 minutes. Sit still and silent in total awareness. Be wide open. Then send all of your energy to your navel, or the space between your eyebrows, for 20 seconds. Relax. Repeat. Again, this is something that you have to feel. But be careful. Don't overdo this one. When you do energy work, it's easy to get jacked up. Even when I sit in stillness and silence in the Zen center, a lot of energy accumulates. Pay attention if you start feeling anxious or manicky. If so, mellow down a bit. You're probably naturally talented for energy work, so just back off the gas pedal a little bit and let it develop more slowly.

Mental Focus

The practice of *pure* mental focus is actually pretty advanced and can be quite difficult. I think it's probably something that very accomplished masters can do. See the stories of teachers like Guru Ramana Maharshi in the Hindu tradition or the 84 Mahasiddhas in the Buddhist Vajrayana traditions for some sense of that that might be like. I'm not super excellent at it, though I have some idea how it works. We use a thought or image in the mind and focus our awareness and intention on it. In the higher tantras, this is done with the image of a deity, such as Green Tara. There are two stages of practice in the Vajrayana, the development stage and the accomplishment stage. In the development, we learn to work with the breath, the mantra, seed syllables such as OM, AH, or HUM, body position, and the image of the deity. In the accomplishment stage, we work with the state of Mahamudra or Great Symbol. That's the state of non-dual oneness, the Tao, Dzogchen, and Samadhi that we've talked about already. These terms, incidentally are not synonymous and come from different systems with varying methodologies. But they kind of point to the same thing.

For our purposes, we'll keep it simple and basic to begin. The simplest way to generate mental focus is to use a mantra. In that sense, we're integrating mind and energy so it's not purely mental. Mantra is speech and speech is energy. Mantra uses breath and breath is energy. The mantra is a vibration. New students always want to know the mantra's meaning, but the meaning cannot be known with words. We work with the vibration and the resultant energy flow as it connects us to our mental state and allow the mantra to transform our energy and our mental state.

Say the mantra out loud enough times for it to feel natural in your silent mind. Sit for 20 minutes in silent, still awareness. Then chant OM, the shortest mantra. You can do any mantra, such as the six syllable mantra of compassion, OM MANI PADME HUM. Take a deep, slow inhale. Let it all out. Pause empty. Notice that. Breathe in deeply. Exhale with the sound of the mantra OM taking up the entire exhale breath. Pause empty. Repeat. Make sure that you get the sound and the vibration deep into your mental space. Close your eyes. Notice empty space. Repeat the OM silently in your mind. At first you can do it mentally while continuing to follow the breath. But make sure to do the mantra only mentally.

If you really want to get into the mantra OM, pronounce it like the real tantric yogis do. It has three parts.

AAAAAHHHH

OOOOOOOO

UUUMMMMM

When you do the mantra verbally, out loud, use your whole mouth and jaw. Over accentuate the movement of the jaw for a while until you really get a sense of using your whole head to sound the mantra. If that's too much, just say OM as I said earlier. That's fine too. But the old yogis do it the extended way because it's said to tune the channels and chakras of energy within your whole brain, body, and energy system.

Words and Meaning

If you'd like to try mental focus with regular words that have meaning, you can definitely do that too. It's a legit meditation technique. If you don't know what word or principle you'd like to use, you can do a brainstorm list of positive words. See if you can create one for every letter of the alphabet. Twenty six words should give you enough to start with. When you've chosen your word, begin a session with ten or twenty minutes of present moment awareness. You can draw this out on paper or with a mind map tool if it helps, but eventually you should take the practice totally inside. Think of your word—love for example. Let the vibration, emotional connection and mental associations resonate within you around that word. But don't get lost or distracted. Bring it up. Pause. Check your body awareness, breath awareness. Focus in on that word again. Then let the associations come. Keep the associations one or two branches away at the most. When your mind digresses, return to the word or even the feeling. I'd say to try this practice for one to two minutes at a time unless you really have super good concentration. Remember not to digress too much. Notice the associated feelings, thoughts, and ideas and then return your mind's focus to the word. Repeat until you understand nothing.

Sample Sessions

Use these sample sessions if you want some structure for individual or group practice. I've placed them in the correct order, but you can change it if you prefer. Feel free to mix and match any way that suits you. Where I've noted a meditation, substitute any meditation from this book. If you get stuck or need a Skype session for yourself or your group, contact me. I'm always happy to lead a retreat or workshop in person as well.

<u>Sample Session One</u>

- Prostations
- Refuge
- Body Awareness Meditation
- Dedication of Merits

<u>Sample Session Two</u>

- Set Intention
- Refuge
- Breath Awareness Meditation
- Dedication of Merits
- Journal

<u>Sample Session Three</u>

- Sky Gazing (with or without a sky)
- Walk with Intention

- Refuge
- Dedication of Merits
- Journal

Sample Session Four

- Offerings
- Refuge
- Koan Practice
- Body Awareness Meditation
- Dedication of Merits

Sample Session Five

- Breath Awareness
- News Practice
- Sit with Intention
- Refuge
- Journal
- Dedication of Merits

Sample Session Six

- Contemplate suffering (attachment, aversion)
- Take Refuge
- Make Offerings
- Dedicate Merits

CONCLUSION

I realize that most people unfamiliar with Dhama have looked at the title and said something like, "Well if there's nothing to gain why would I be interested in that?" If that's you, and you've managed to read the whole book, then I'm going to guess that you've got an interest in what the Buddha taught. I don't think people read books like this if they don't have an interest. My teacher quotes the Buddha as saying that among the characteristics of practitioners that are necessary to transcend suffering, interest *and* participation are the most important. Without that, there is nothing.

You might think, "This is a whole lot of double talk and the author is just trying to be clever." But the truth is that there is ultimately nothing to gain from Buddhist practice. There are a whole lotta things to let go of though. And when we do, we find that we've been sitting on the treasure the whole time. The wisdom that there is nothing substantial in the universe and that we can't get any more of anything because ultimately there is nothing *is* the treasure. But we can't get to it on the raft of our intellect. That said, we have to use our intellect to read words and hear teachings and learn practices that will ultimately become unnecessary, like spiritual training wheels.

So why do I say that this is a how-to book? Because it is. There are enough practices in the preceding chapters that you can teach yourself how to "realize emptiness," as Buddhists say. We learned about our condition, and how to learn more about our condition by practicing awareness, intention and focus. But we do so with the knowledge of samsara, what it means to be a yogi, how suffering manifests, how to take refuge, purify karma, create merit and let it all pass by, like clouds in the sky.

New students have a hard time with the mental battle of the often paradoxical language of Dharma. But at some point, if we practice seriously, we learn that we can "drop the rock and join the parade." We might put down our weapons and find ourselves weeping with the true heart of compassion. As my teacher, Venerable Robina Courtin says, there are two wings to the dharma, the wing of compassion and the wing of wisdom. There is no separation of the two. We can't realize emptiness without finding ourselves in absolute compassion and we wouldn't be able to dwell in the heart of the Buddha's teachings on compassion unless we realize that there is ultimately nothing, at all to gain from Buddhist practice.

The Great Heart of Wisdom (Prajnaparamita) Sutra sums it all up in one line. Feel free to chant this one, silently or aloud, alone or with the trillions of suffering beings who want to transcend samsara, with words or from a place beyond words:

TAYATA OM GATE GATE PARASAMGATE
BODHI SVAHA

May you and all beings find lasting freedom and true happiness and be of maximum benefit to as many suffering beings as there are in the infinite oceans of samsara until every last one is enlightened.

Until then, be well.

-d

Darren Littlejohn

Summer, 2016

San Diego, CA

AUTHOR'S NOTE

So what have you gained from reading this book and doing the practices? I'll tell you what I've gained. I wrote this book based on a talk that was based on meditations I'd been teaching for the past couple of years. Those meditations were based on how I practice in an integrated way with everything I've learned from 32 years of AA, meditation, hundreds of retreats, workshops, gatherings, yoga classes, books, dreams, nightmares. This book is as much for me as it is for you. It's a guide. I use these tools. Use them yourself. Share with friends. Be on a path, bring others onto a path. Take refuge in something beyond concepts. Set the aspirations and dedicate the merits to fully liberate the endless oceans of suffering beings caught in the infinite cycle of samsara. When you understand the title with your body, speech, and mind, send me an email. I'll come take teachings from you.

OM AH HUM

GLOSSARY

Asana: posture

Buddha: enlightened being

Dharma: teachings, truths, practices

Dharmakaya: enlightened mental dimension

Dzogchen: path of self-liberation

Karma: cause

Mantra: sacred words, syllables, phrases

Mahayana: Great Vehicle

Meditation: placing the mind on an object

Mudra: sacred hand positions

Nirmanakaya: enlightened physical dimension

Pranayama: directed breathing practice

Pratyahara: focused awareness from deep withdrawing of the senses

Samsara: infinite cycle of birth, sickness, old age and death

Siddhi: attainment

Sambhogakaya: enlightened energy dimension

Sangha: spiritual community

Sutra: path of renunciation, the documents related to the path

Tantra: path of transformation, the documents related to the path

Vajrayana: diamond vehicle, path of tantra in Tibetan Buddhism

Yoga: practices of being non-dual with our real nature

Yogi: anyone who takes the path seriously

RESOURCES

Foundation for the Preservation of the Mahayana Tradition

International Dzogchen Community

Padmasambhava Center James Low

Chogyal Namkhai Norbu Rinpoche

His Holiness Dalai Lama

My other sites:

the12stepbuddhist.com

darrenlittlejohn.com

upgradeyourvibration.com

Also by Darren Littlejohn

The 12-Step Buddhist

Perfect Practice

The Power of Vow